SEASCAPE
PAINTINGS & POETRY

MICHAEL CREESE

Copyright © 2021 by Michael Creese
All rights reserved.

No part of this publication or the information in it may be quoted or reproduced in any form without prior written permission from the copyright holder.

Acknowledgments

I would like to thank Stacy Shaneyfelt for carefully editing this manuscript, and for her suggestions on image placement and overall tone.

Written and illustrated by Michael Creese.

Part 1
Gentle

Sunrise in Florida, with shades of cobalt blue, coral, amber, and violet.

There is no witness to this beautiful event, except the Earth and sky.

The Sun, lovingly gazing down, like an artist painting a canvas with impermeable light.

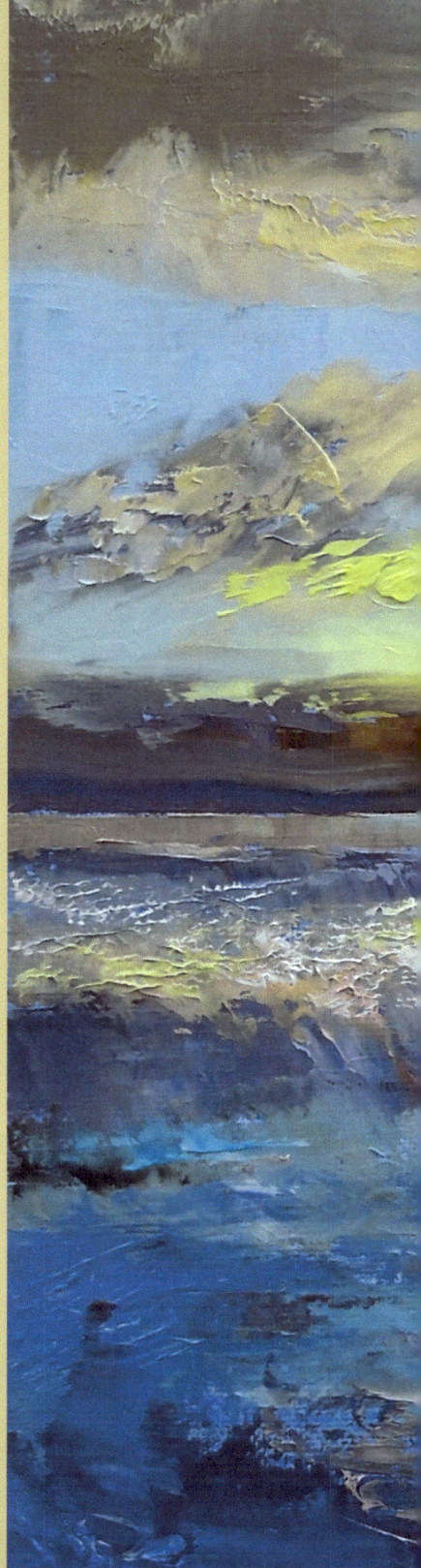

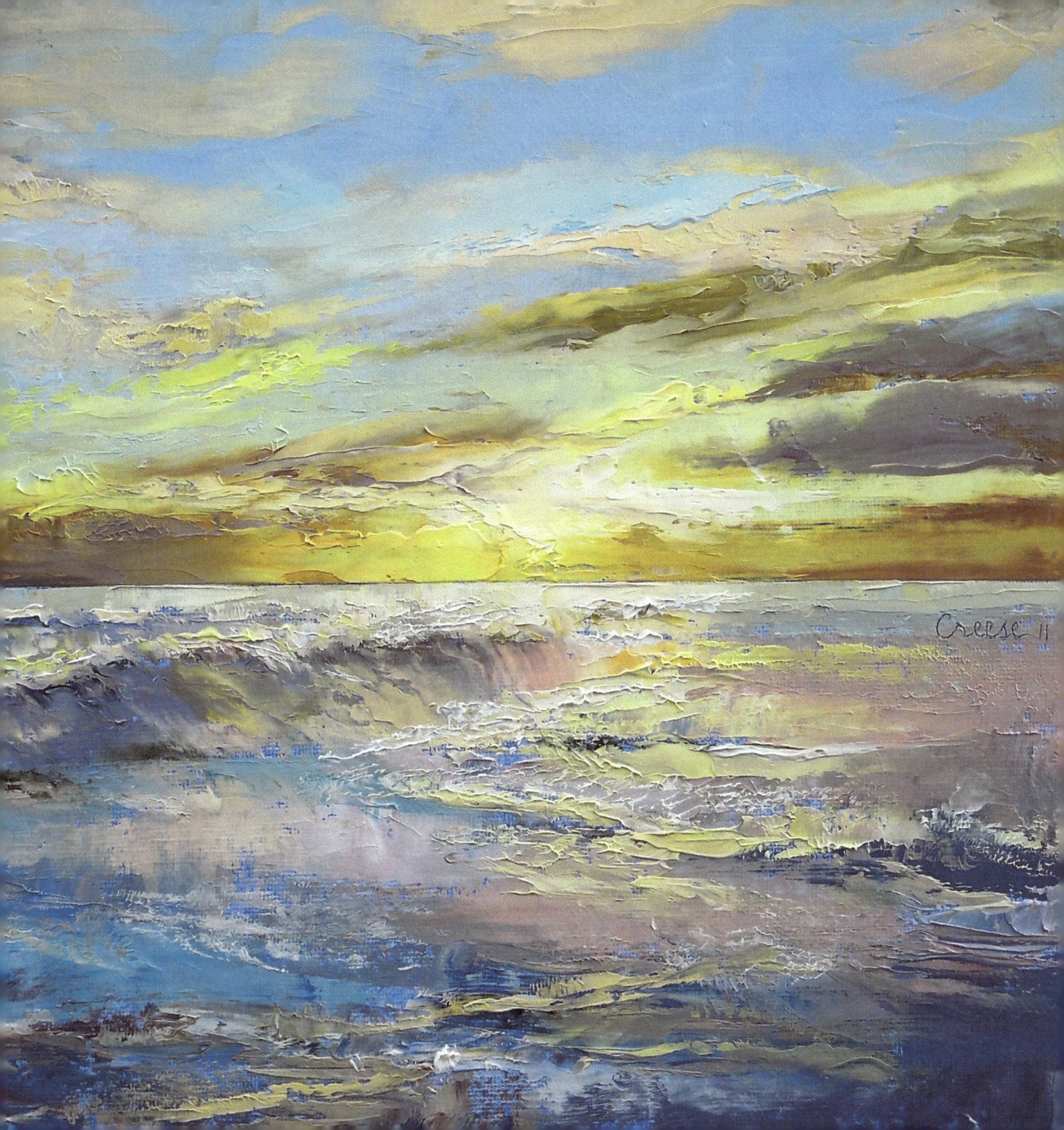

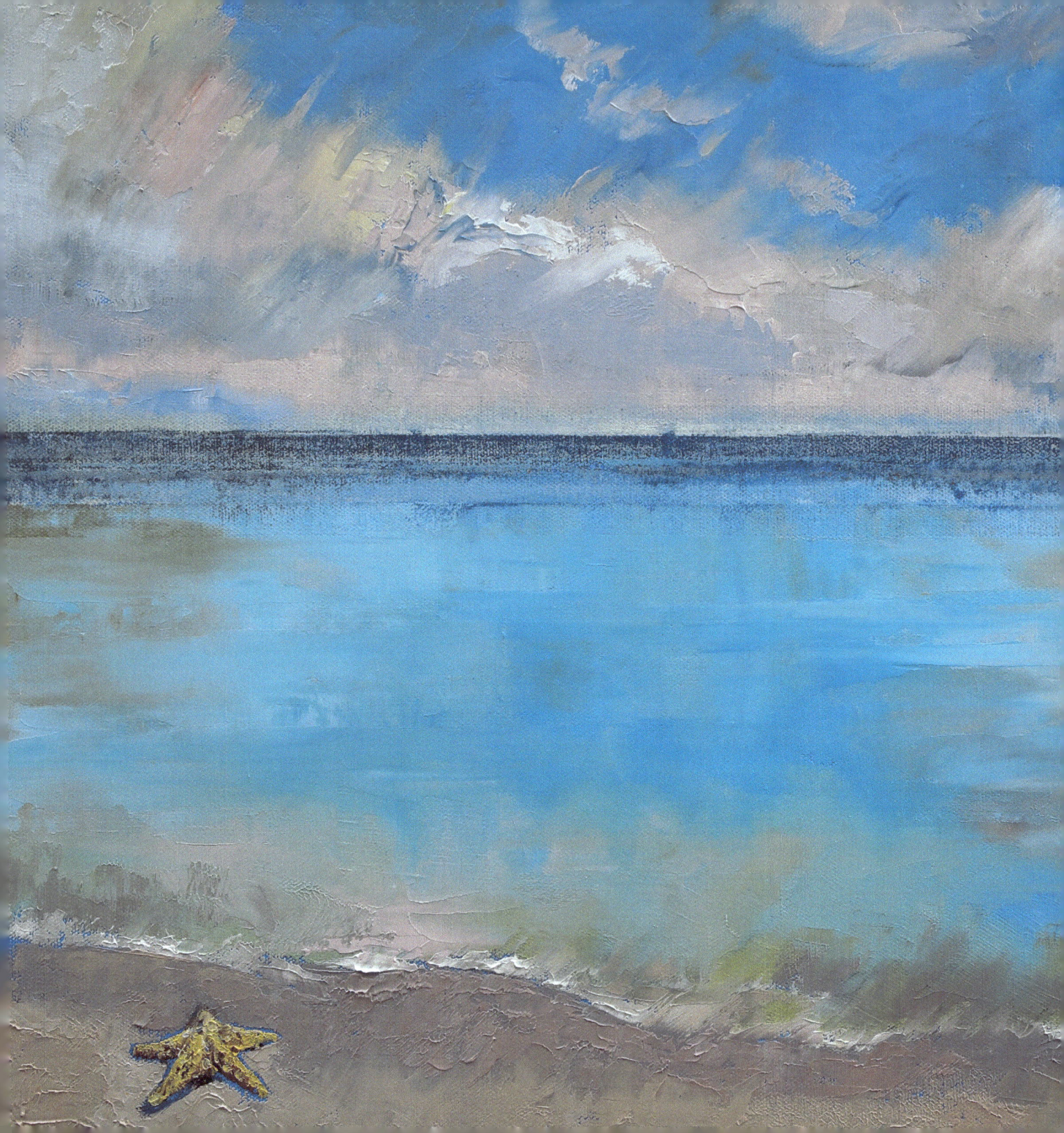

The Caribbean Sea, with clear blue reflections and shimmering, gossamer clouds.

Motionless, were it not for a single starfish sprawling in the sand, just beyond the shoreline.

Nature is its own metronome, untethered from time.

Mount Fiji rises up above a calm blue lake.

Her white, snow-capped peak glimmering in the basin.

Like a young Narcissus, captivated by her own reflection.

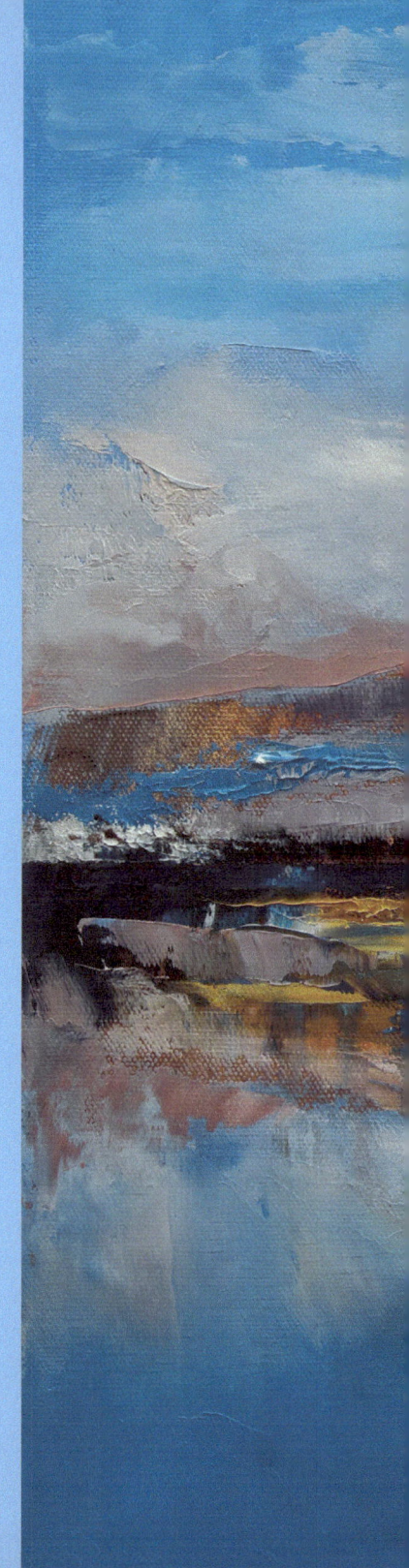

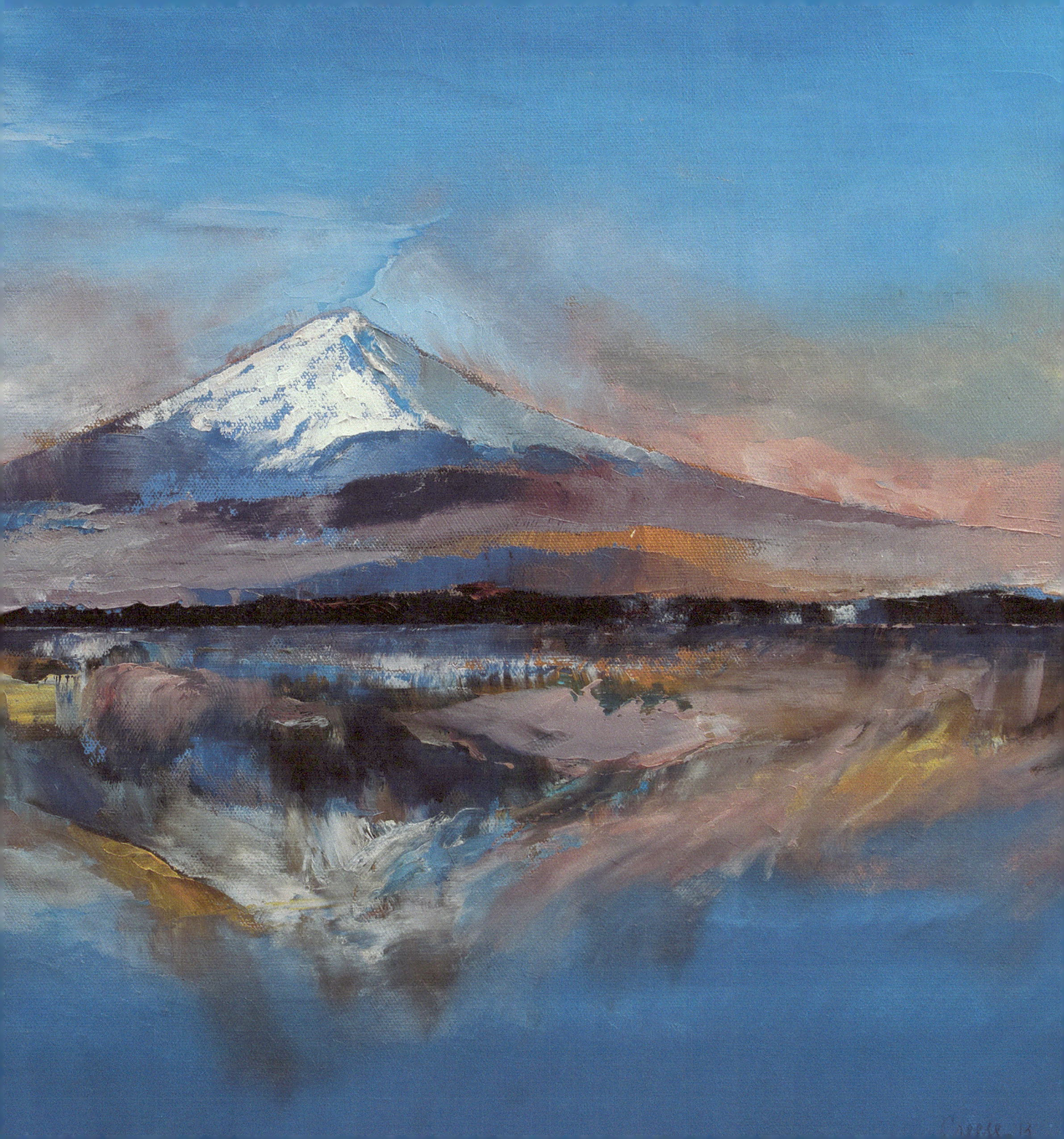

A beautiful parfait sunset off the coast of Africa, with shimmering gold and sepia tones.

Behold, an abstract painting with a limitless palette!

Created by the Sun from the remnants of another dying star.

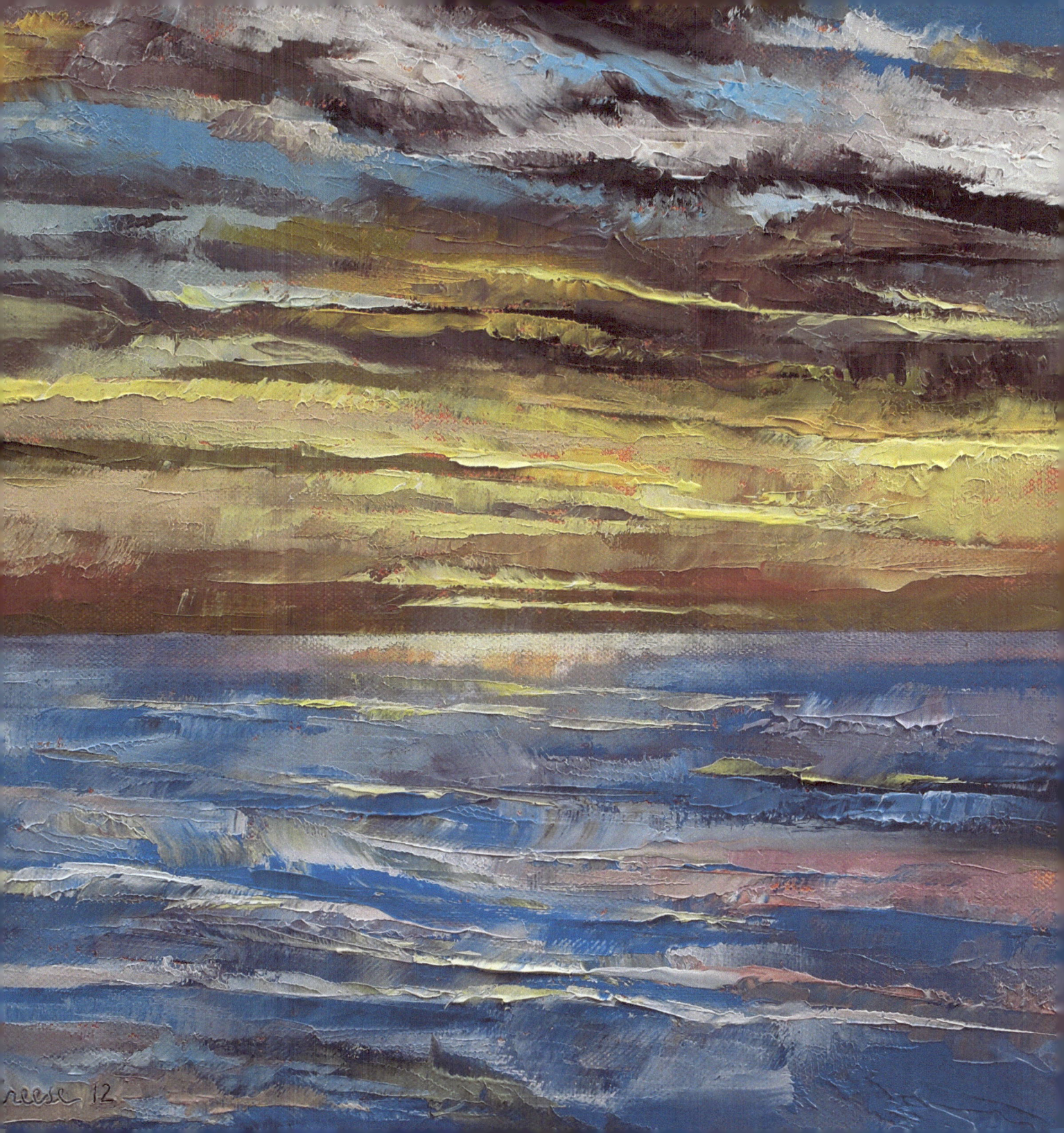

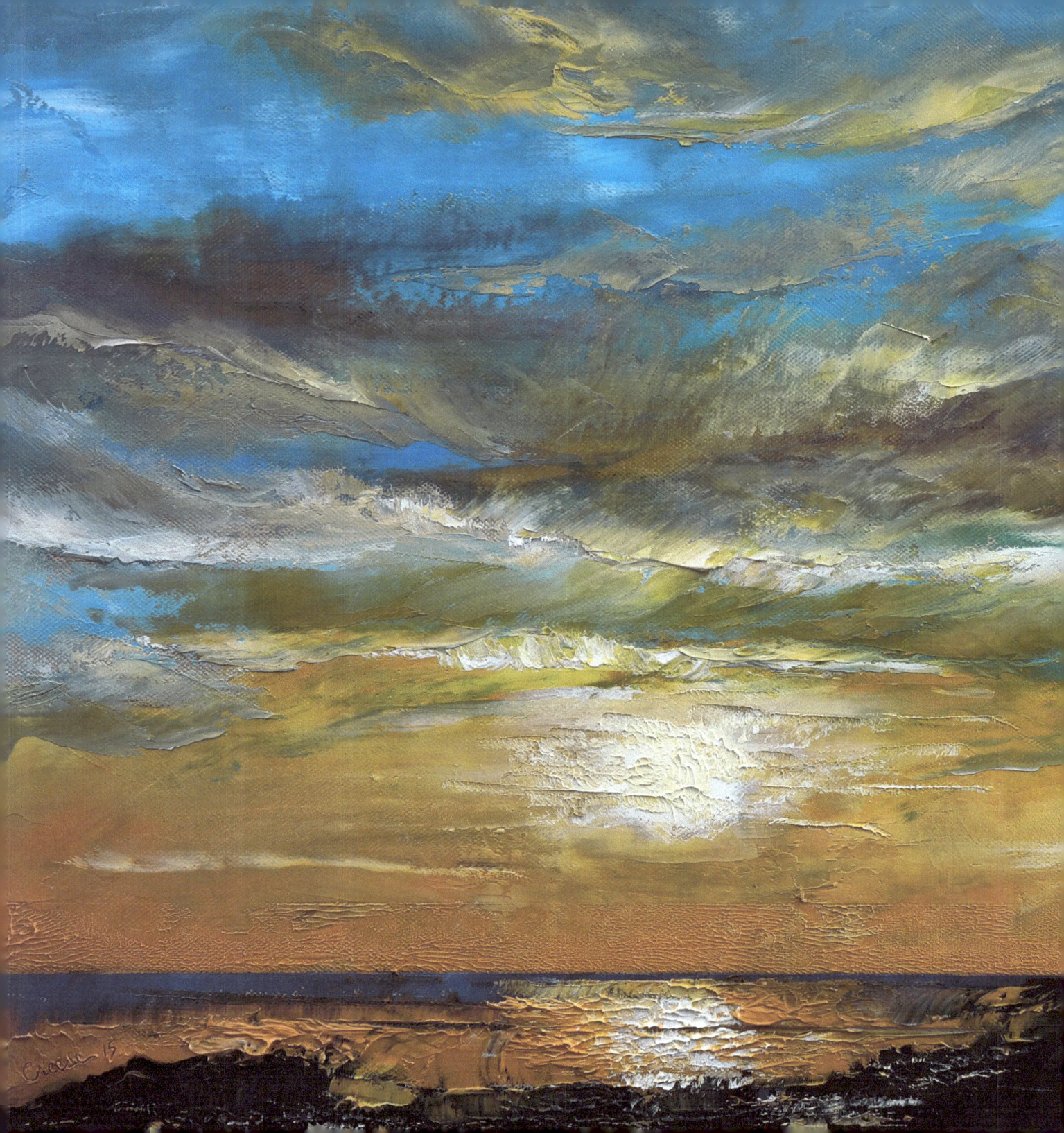

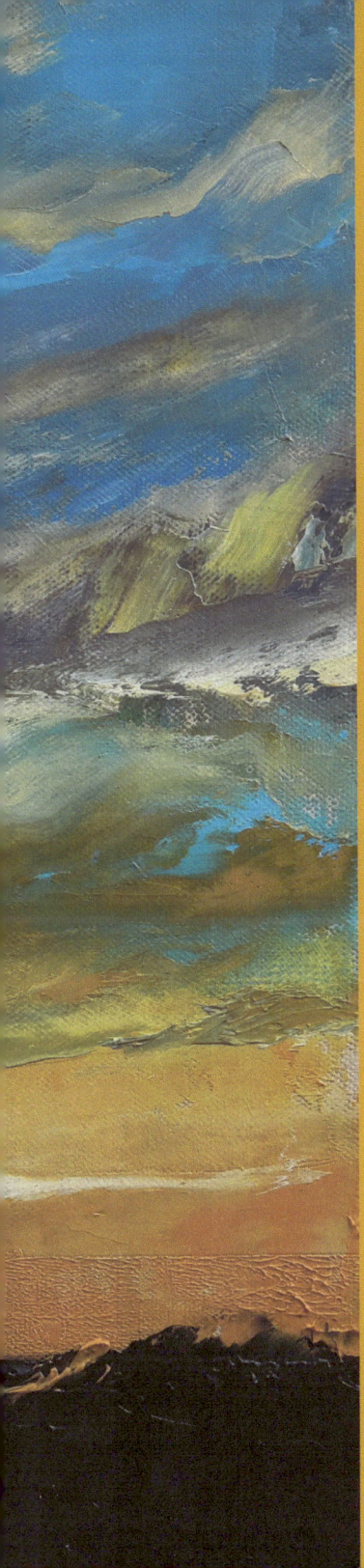

Hawaiian sunset in shades of tiger orange and cerulean blue.

Black lava sand blanketing the shore paints a natural picture frame to an effusion of mandarin and tangerine.

Key West, Florida sunset with a beautiful kaleidoscope of vibrant colors.

Sailing out on the ocean with a gentle breeze, as if pirouetting on glass.

Brushstrokes of color race across the sky.

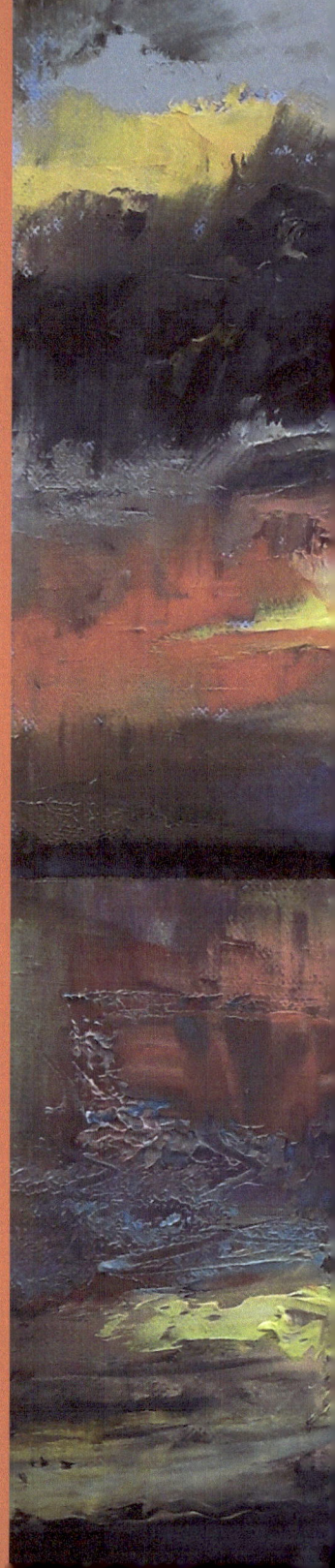

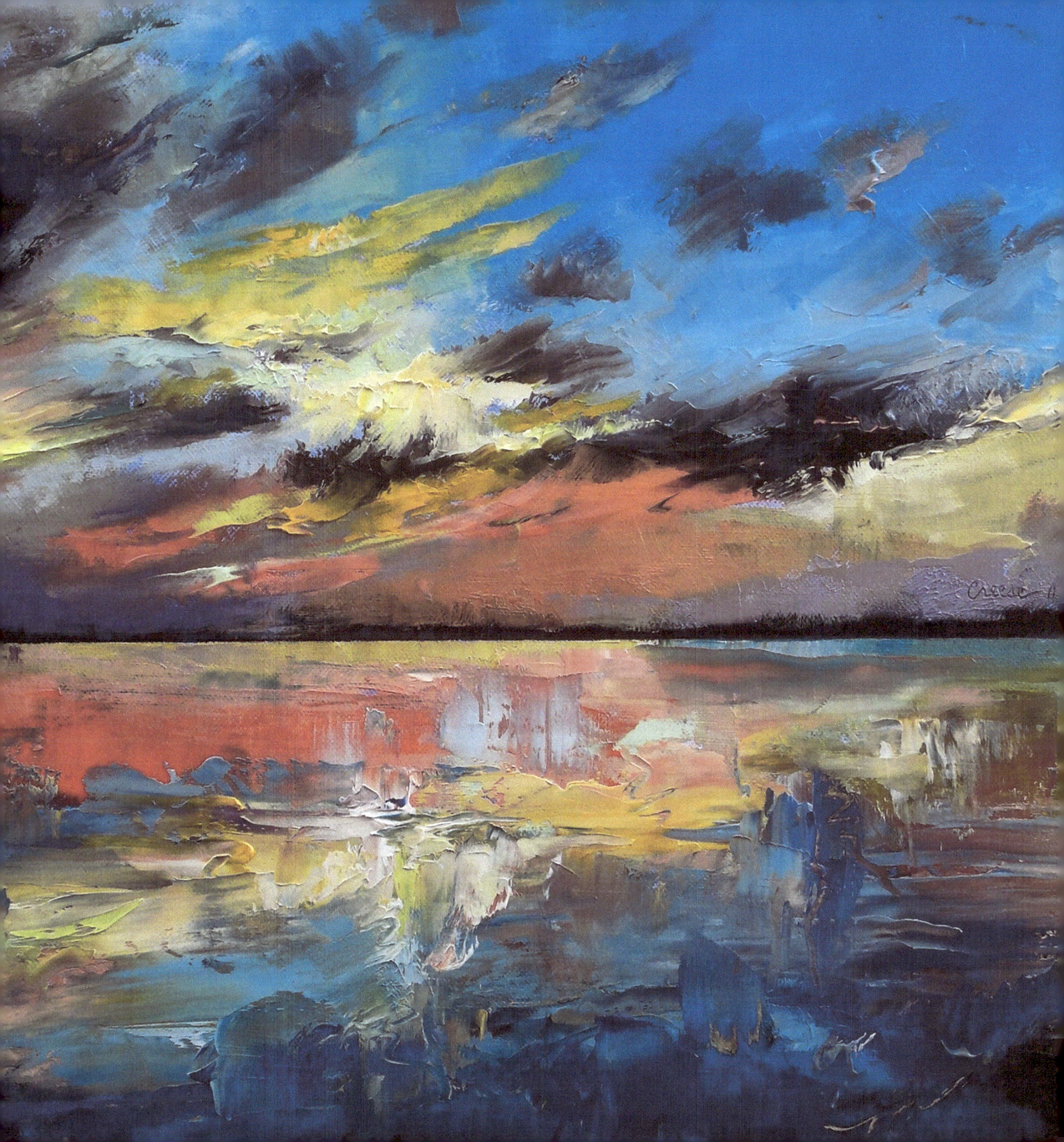

Deep blue Caribbean sunset, with muted colors and the promise of another day.

Ultramarine blue with gold embellishments, as midnight fast approaches.

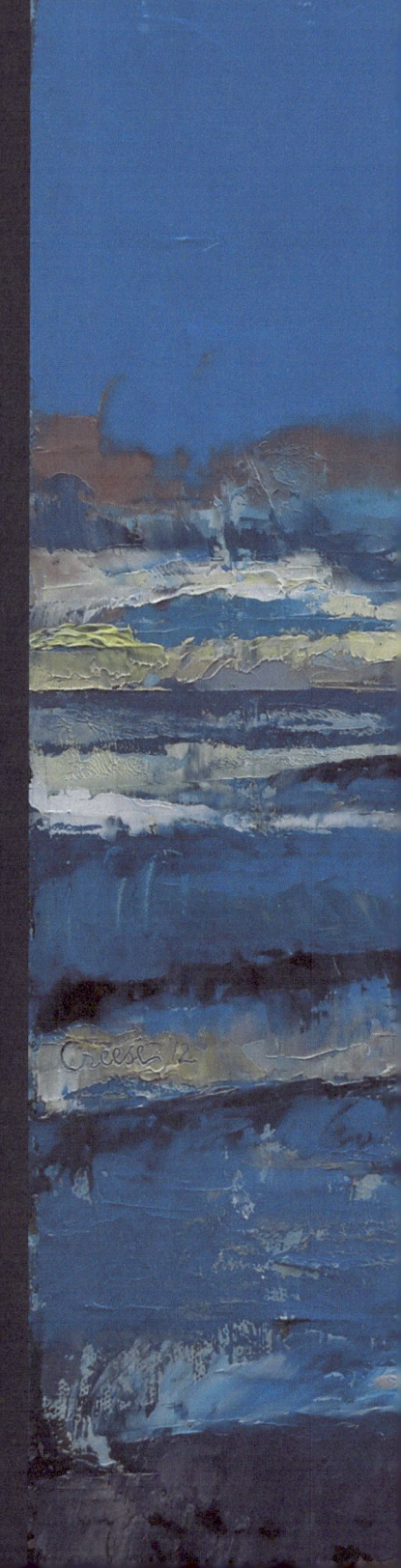

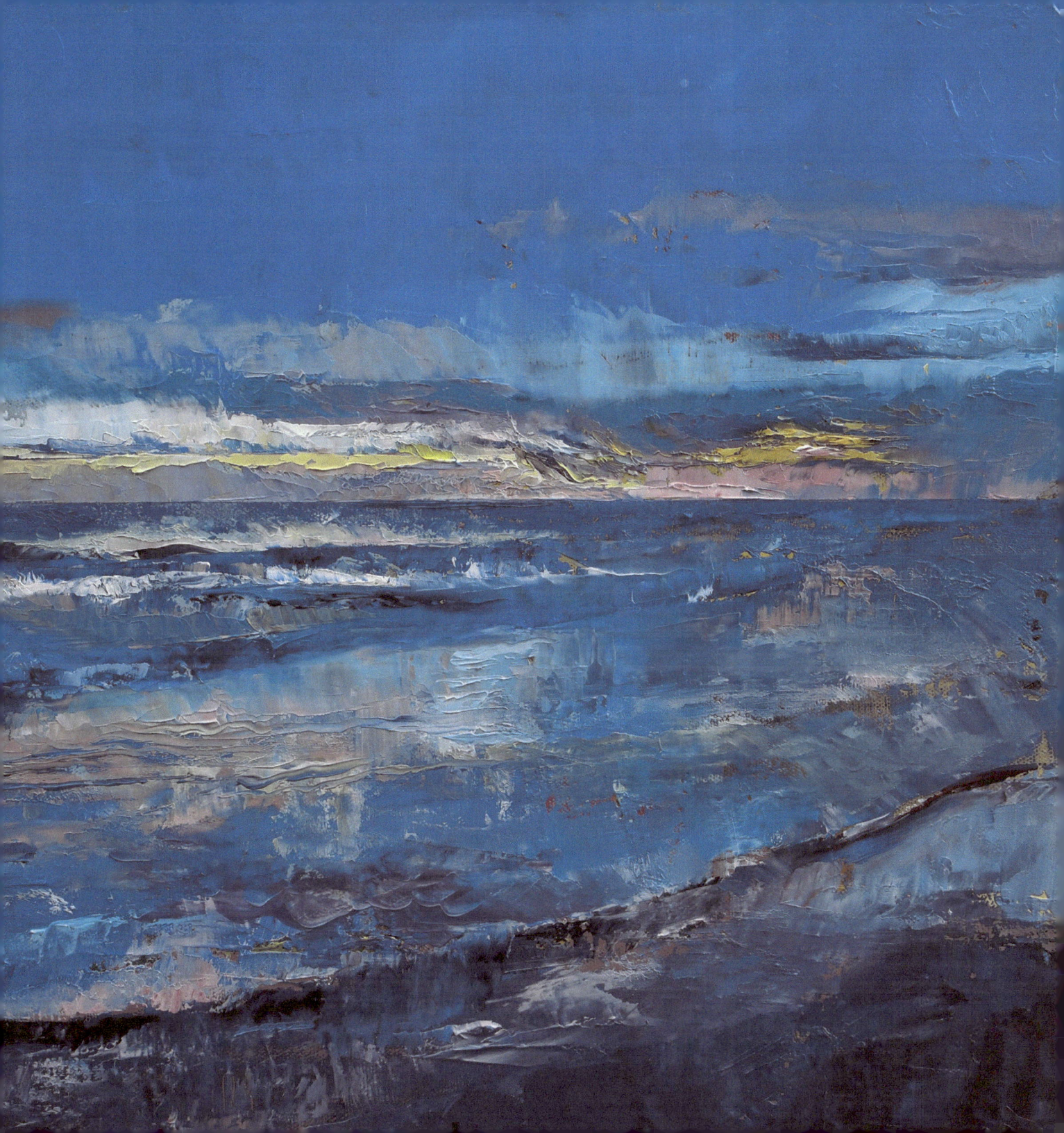

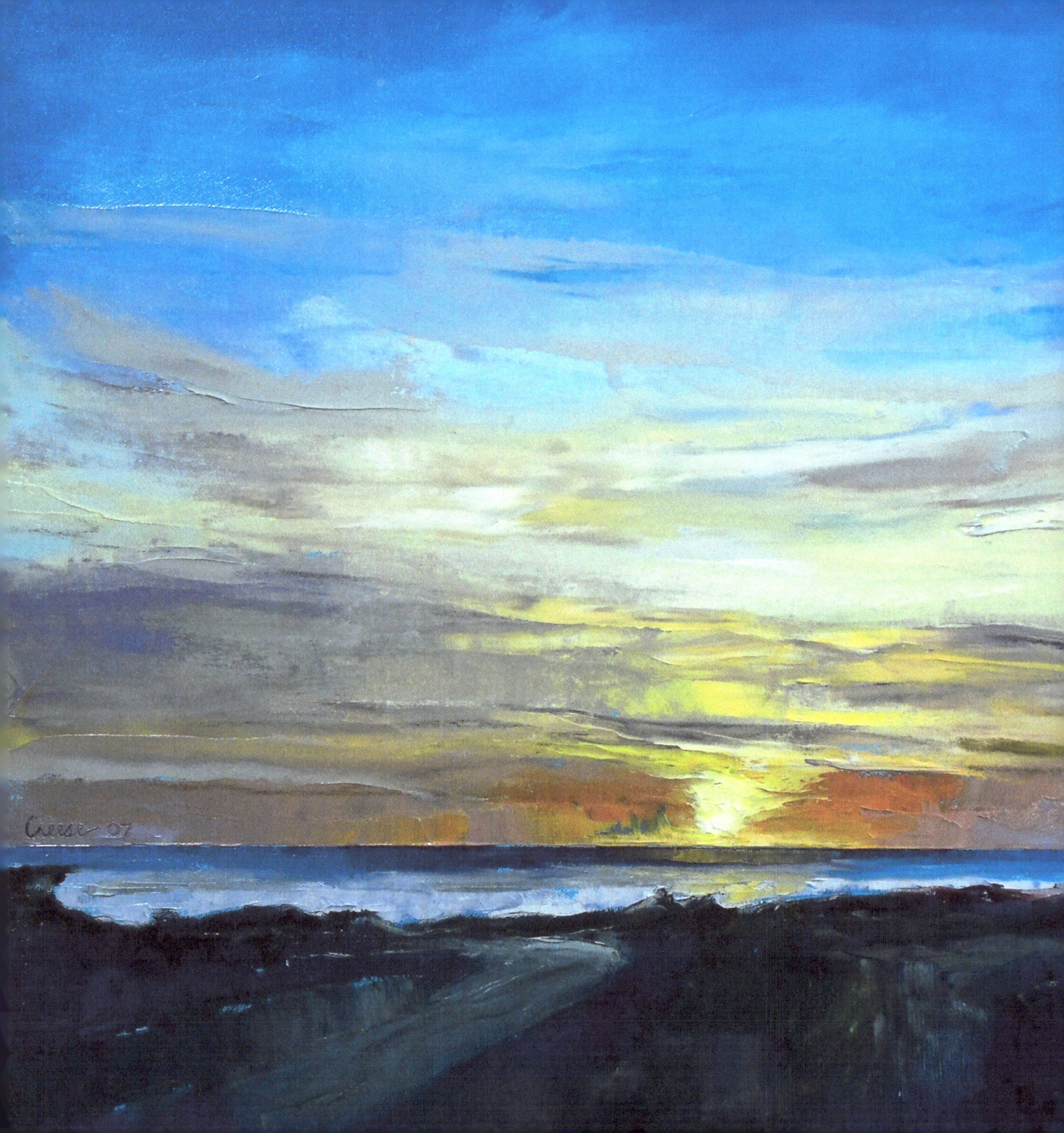

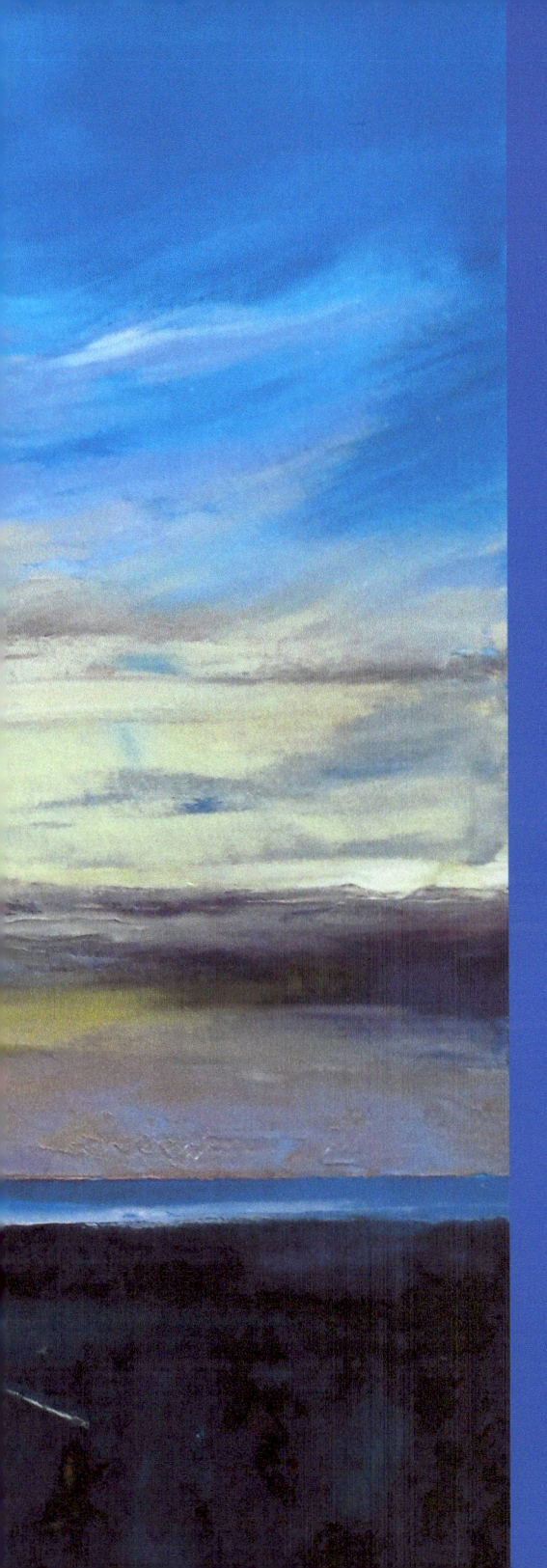

Midnight Sun barely rises over the Arctic Sea to fill the sky with light.

Painted in muted colors and sweeping gestures by the Sun.

A long, dark winter with little warmth, except for the affirmation of Spring.

Part 2
Romantic

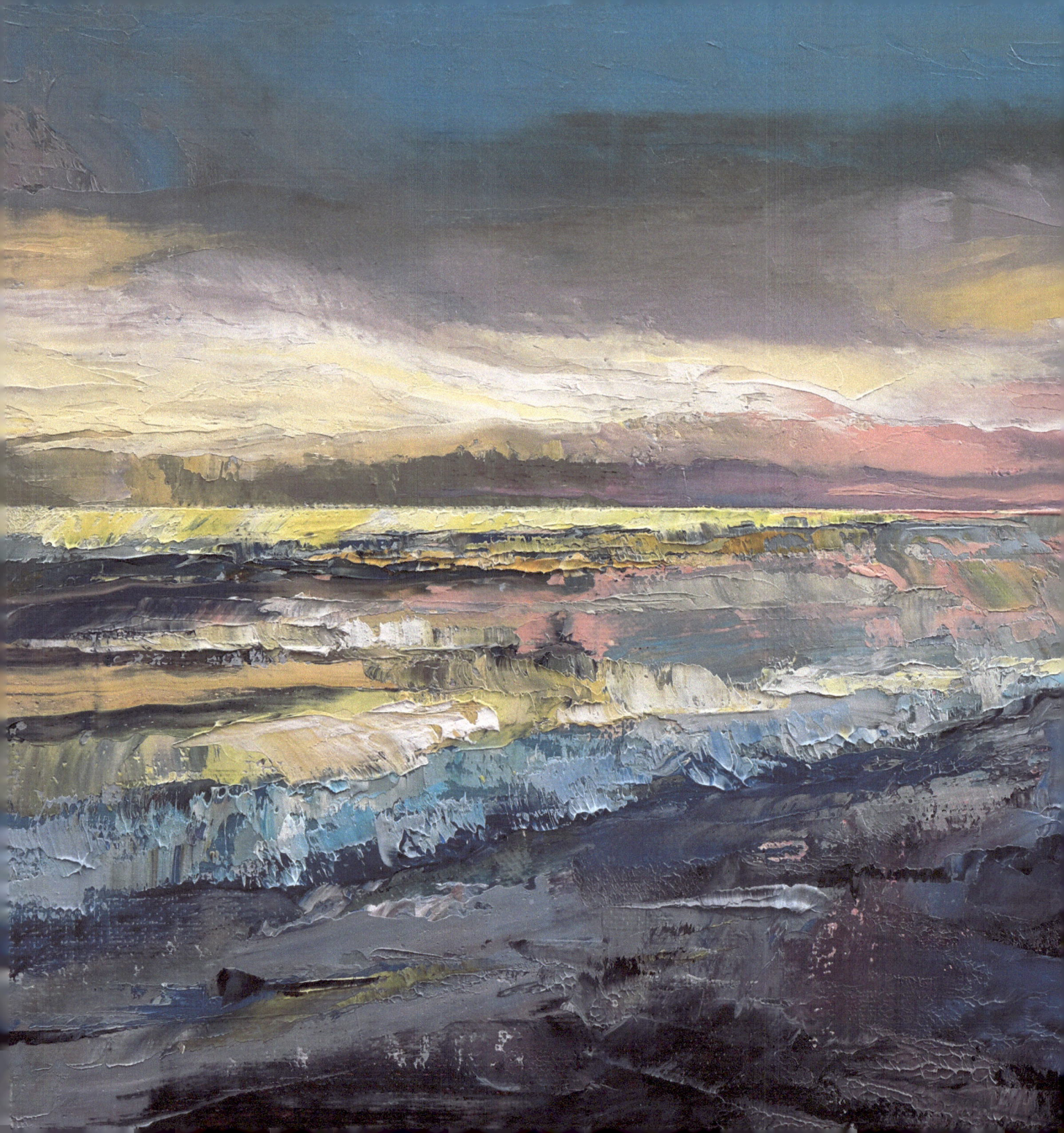

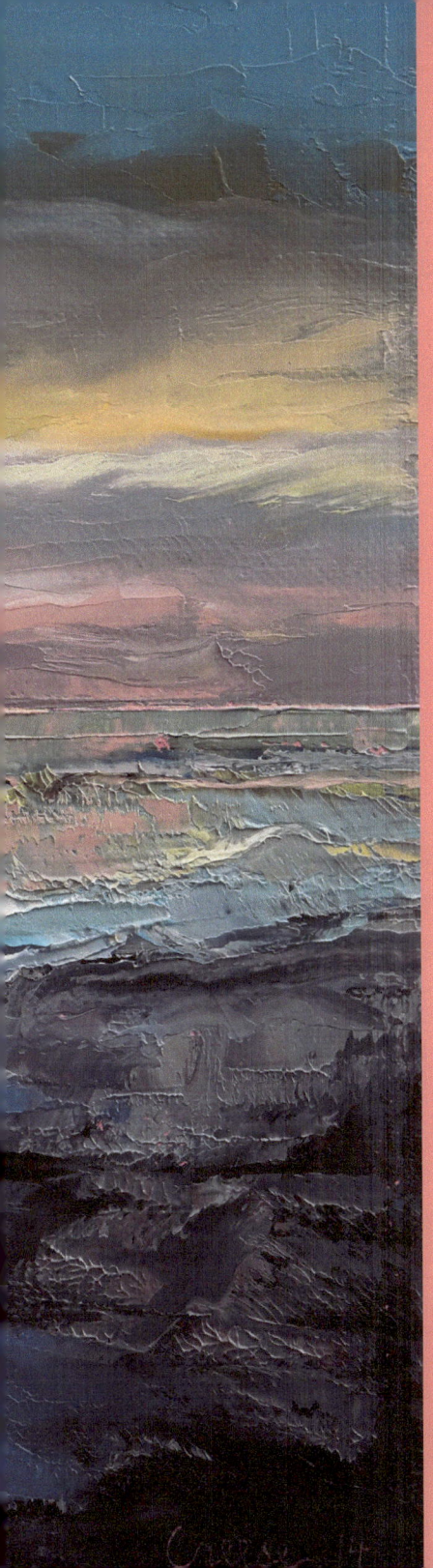

Heavenly shores along the coast of Oregon, with basalt steps and pastel blue overtones.

Is it possible Heaven could resemble this?

The light so subtle in the evening tones, reminiscent of a time lost to the ages.

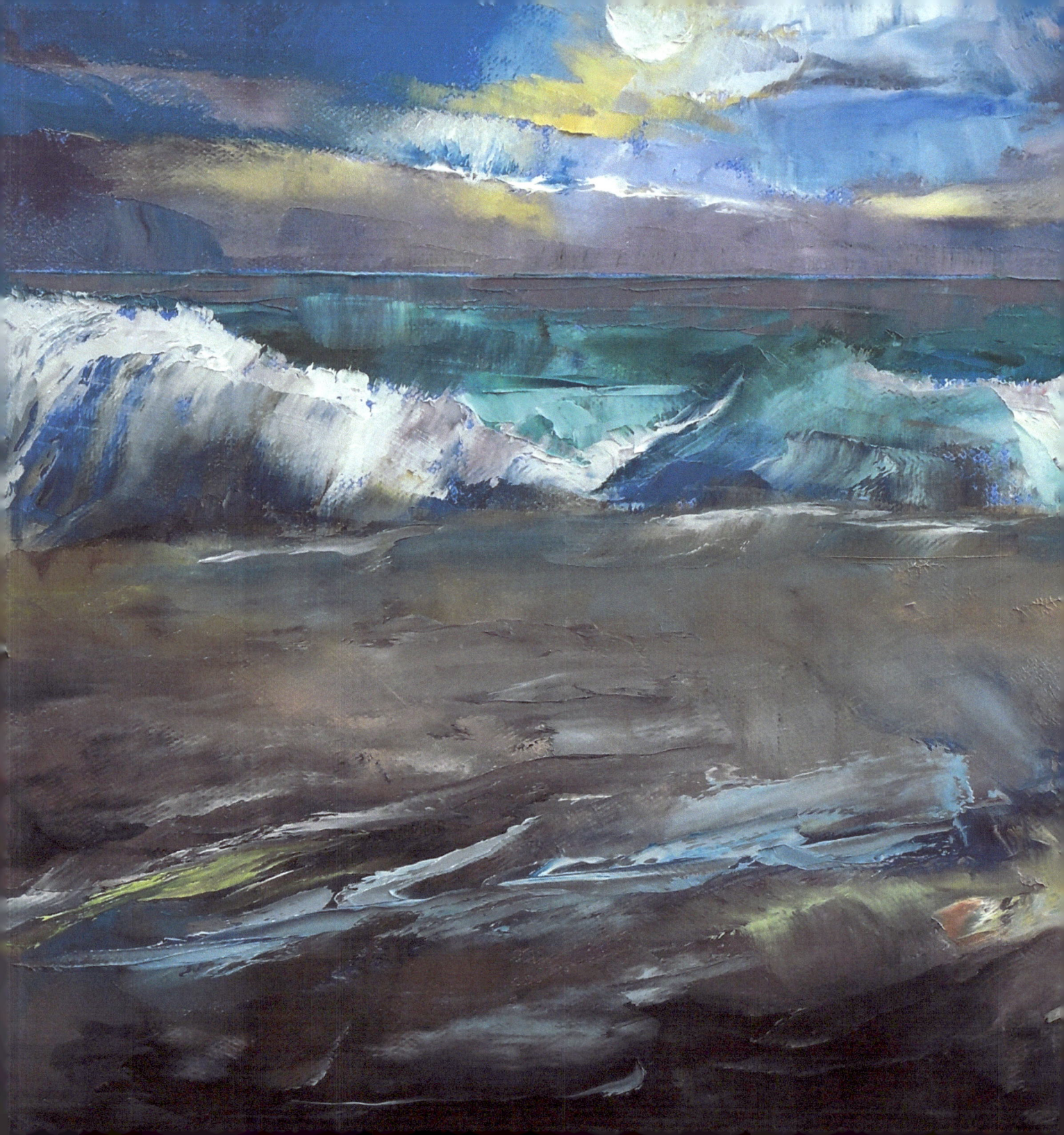

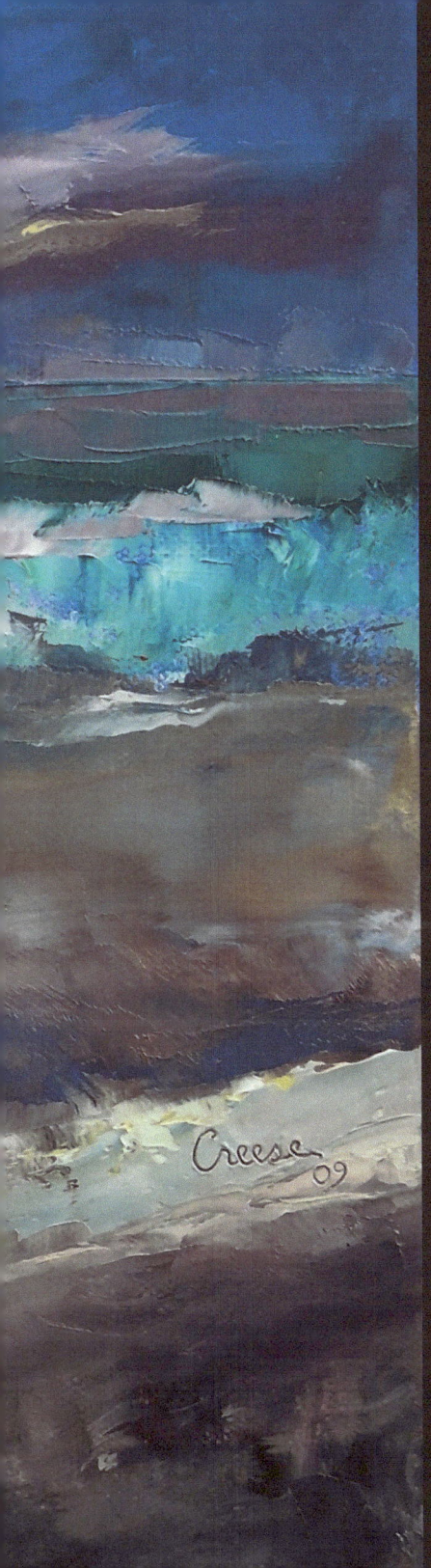

Moonlit waves along the Treasure Coast collapse onto the shore, as the Moon ignites the green gossamer of ocean tides.

No love is comparable.

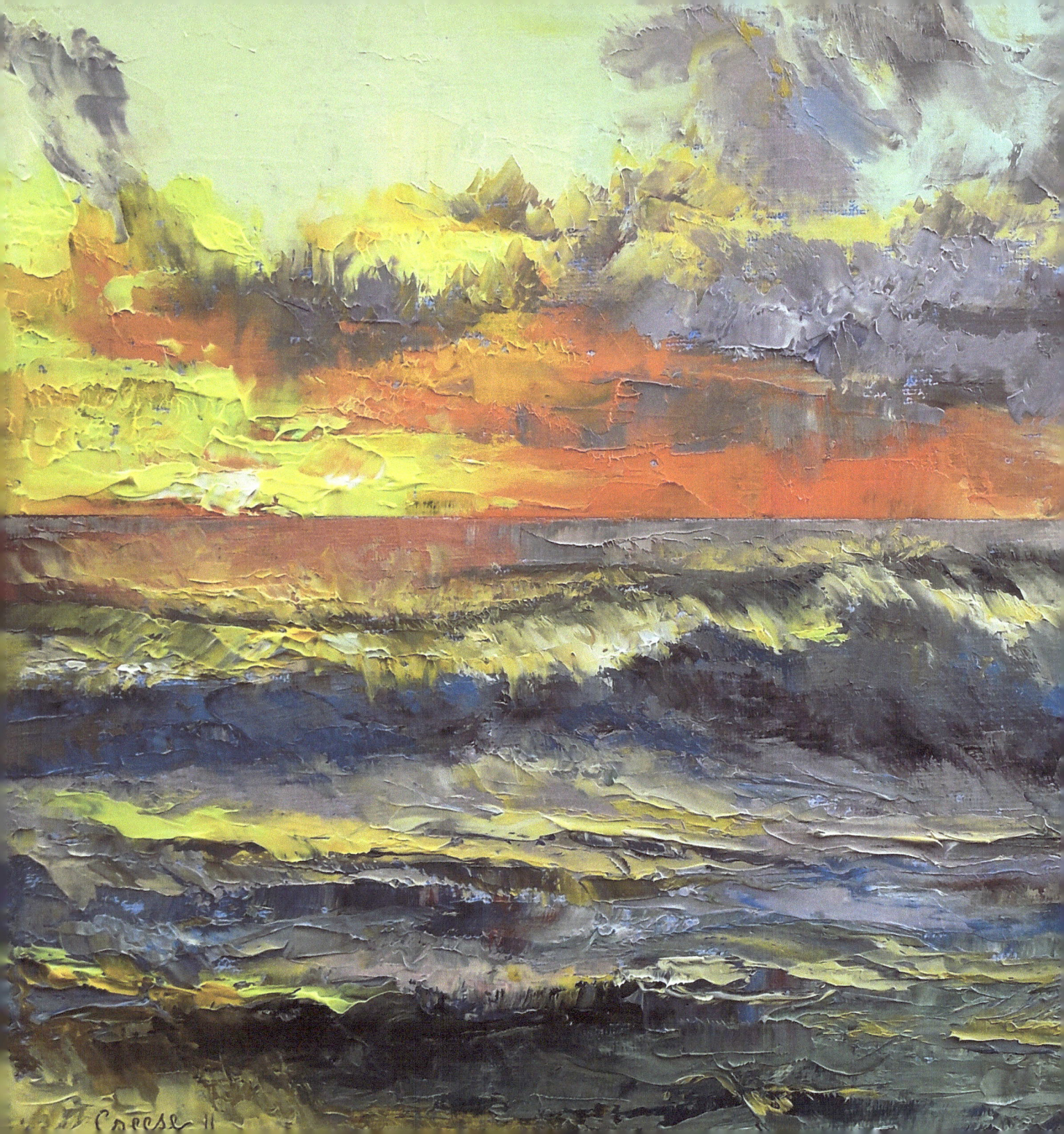

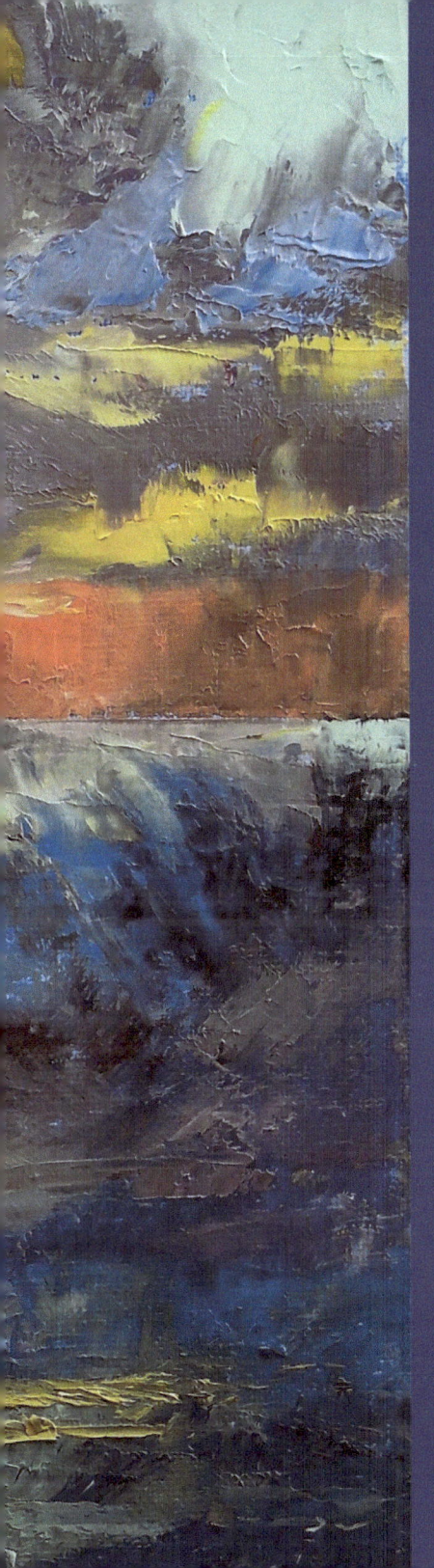

California waves pound the shore, gold and glittery forms in the fading light.

The power of the waves so immense, forming the repetitions of a beating heart in the throes of love.

Tropical sunsets, on the Caribbean island of Saint Martin, are like no other place on Earth.

So difficult to describe in a rational way.

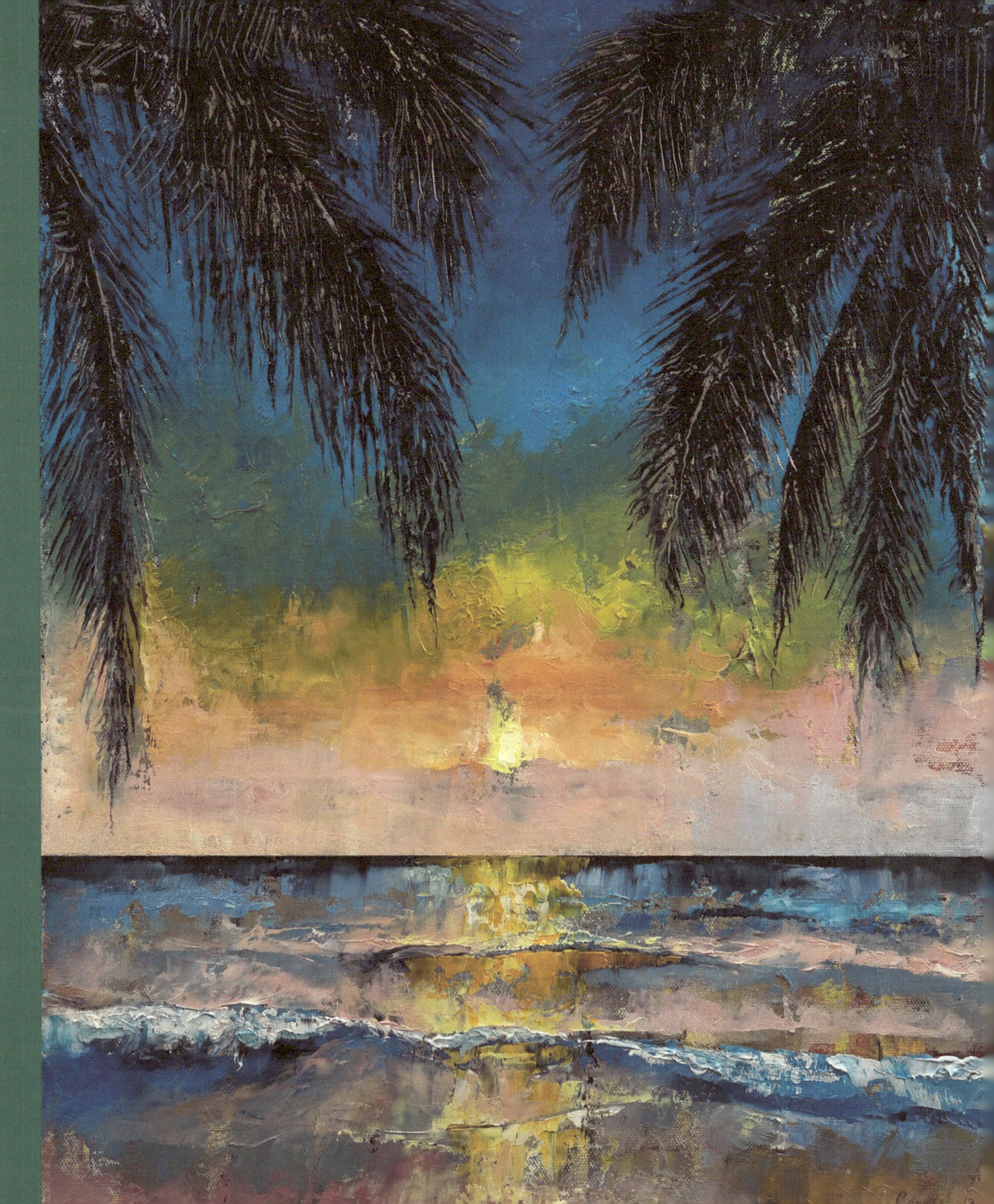

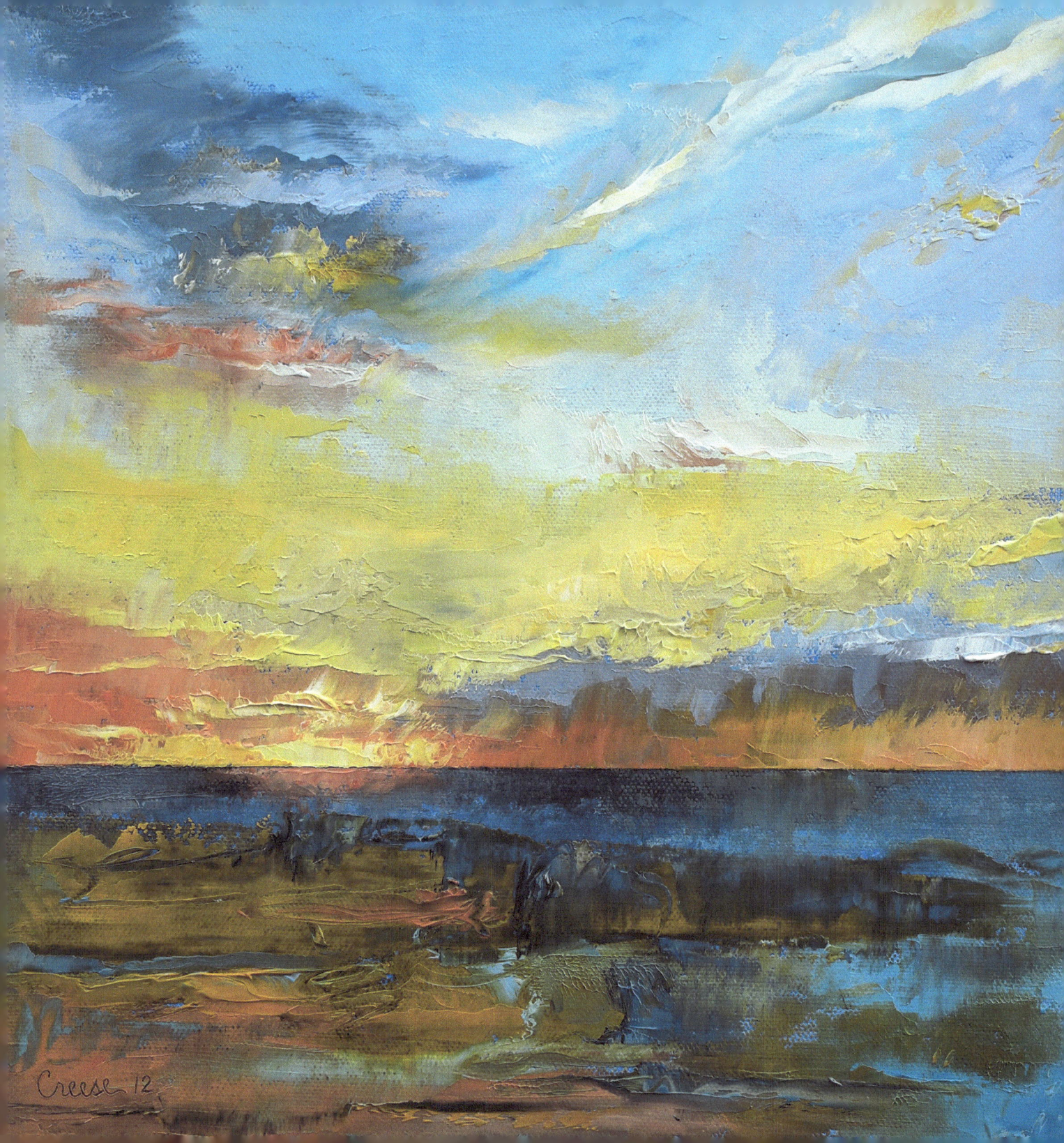

Turquoise and gold ribbons drift effortlessly in the sky over The Bahamas.

A fleeting glimpse of something that resembles all the light and laughter in this world.

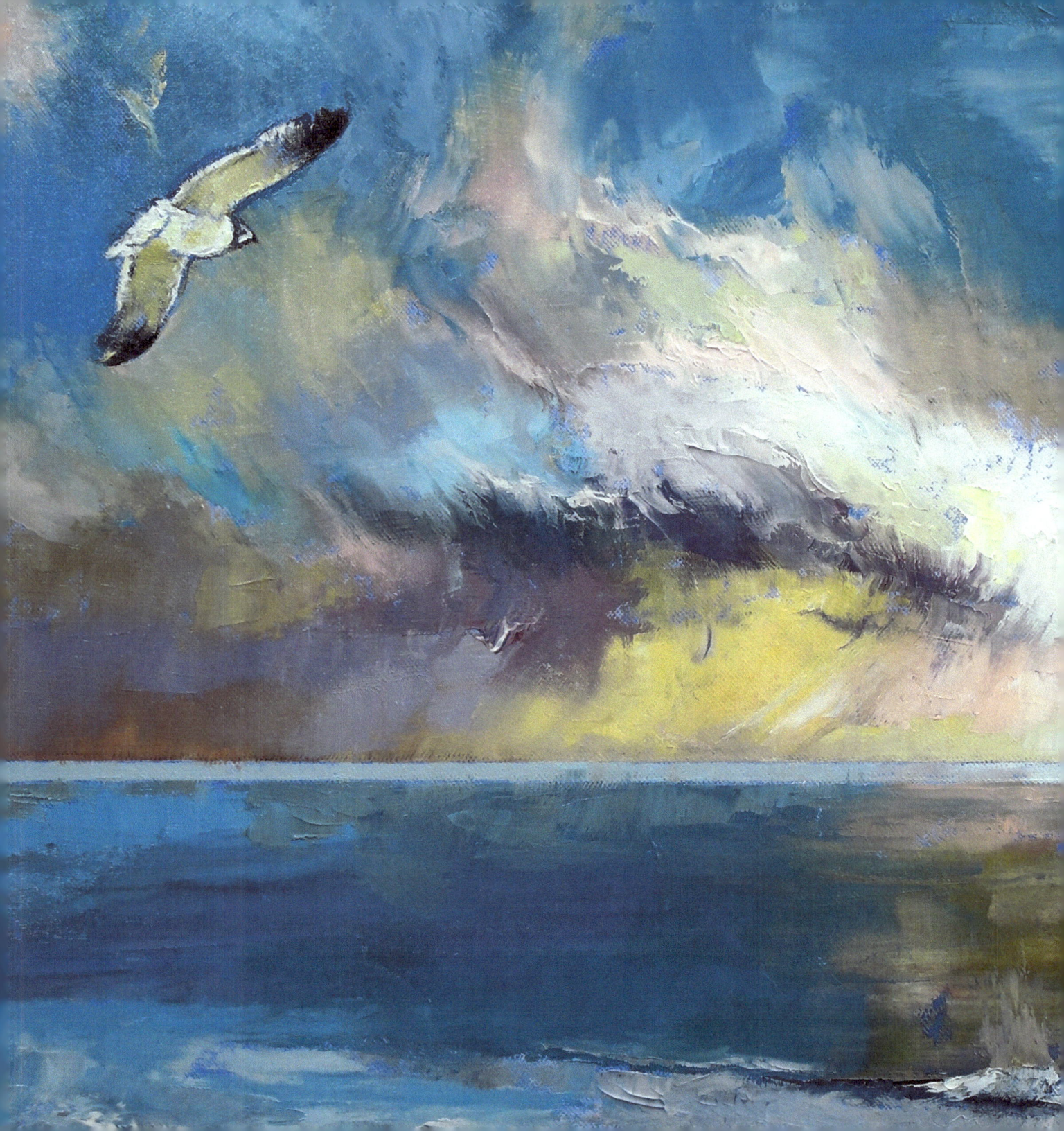

Eternal light over the ocean, as clouds form the wings of an Angel.

A seagull's journey has just begun, as waves caress the shore.

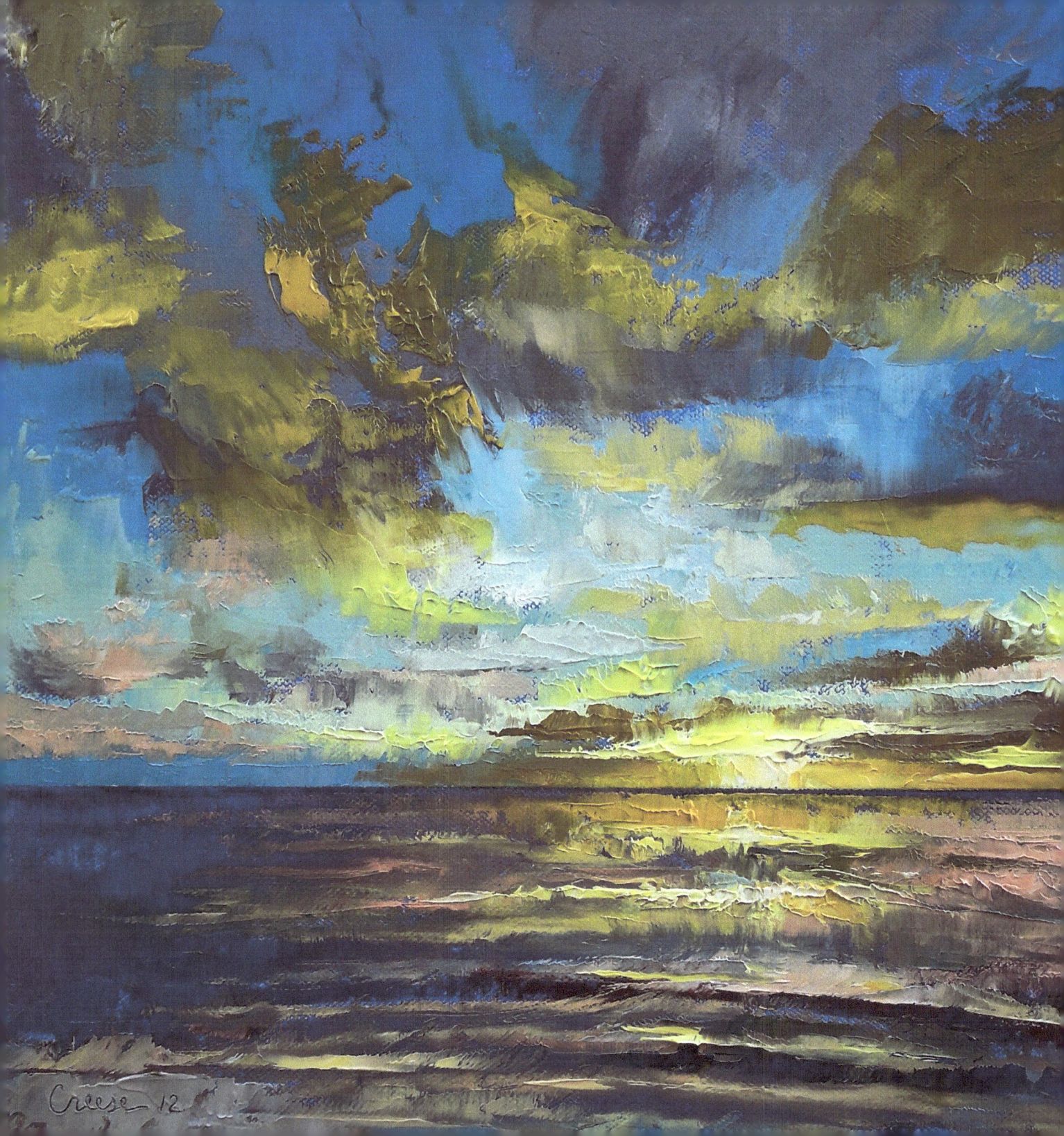

Key Largo sunsets will take the breath away.

The clouds take on so many different shapes on this beautiful stage.

Relentless waves nudging the shore, feel like a memory from an ancient place and time.

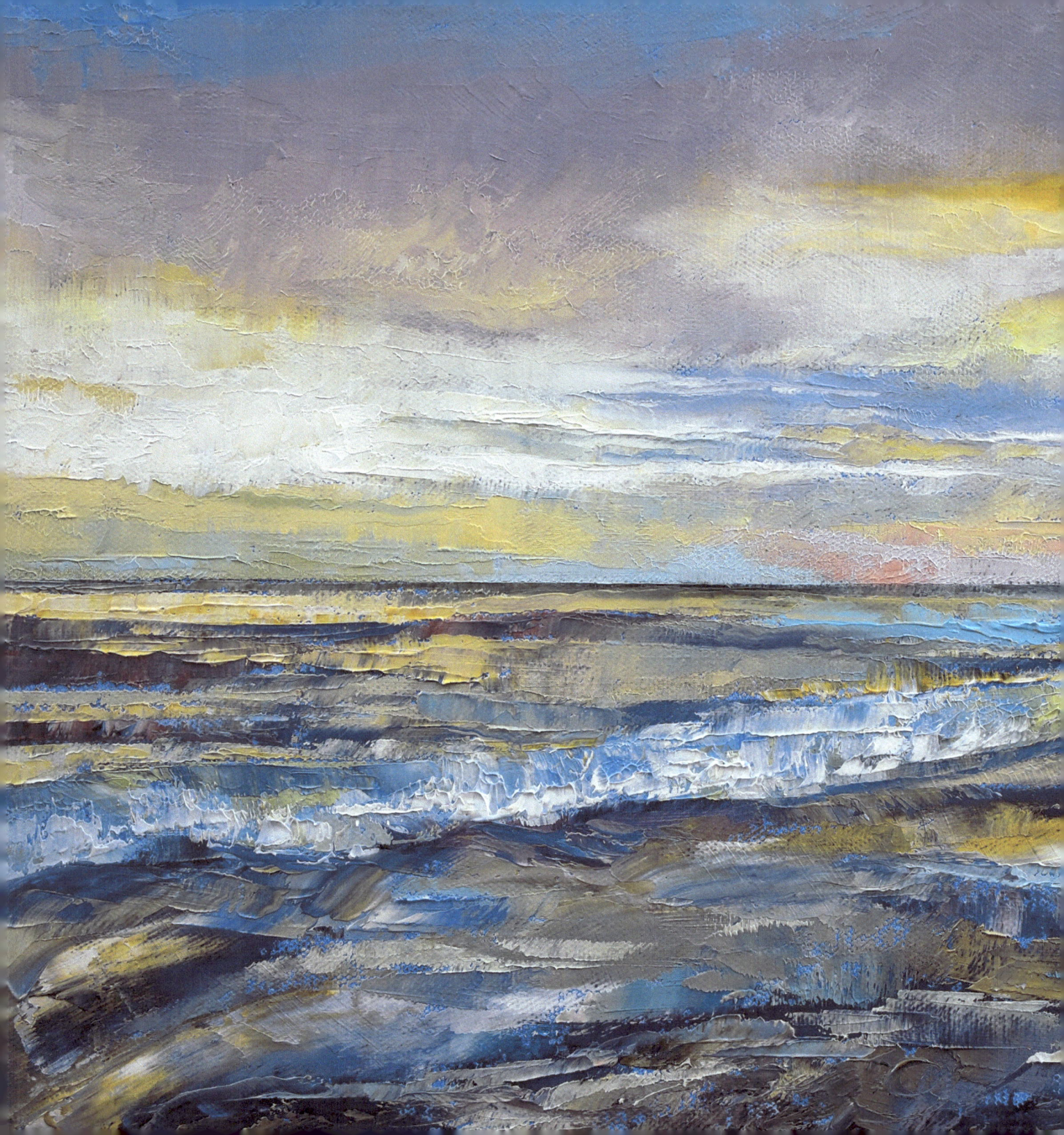

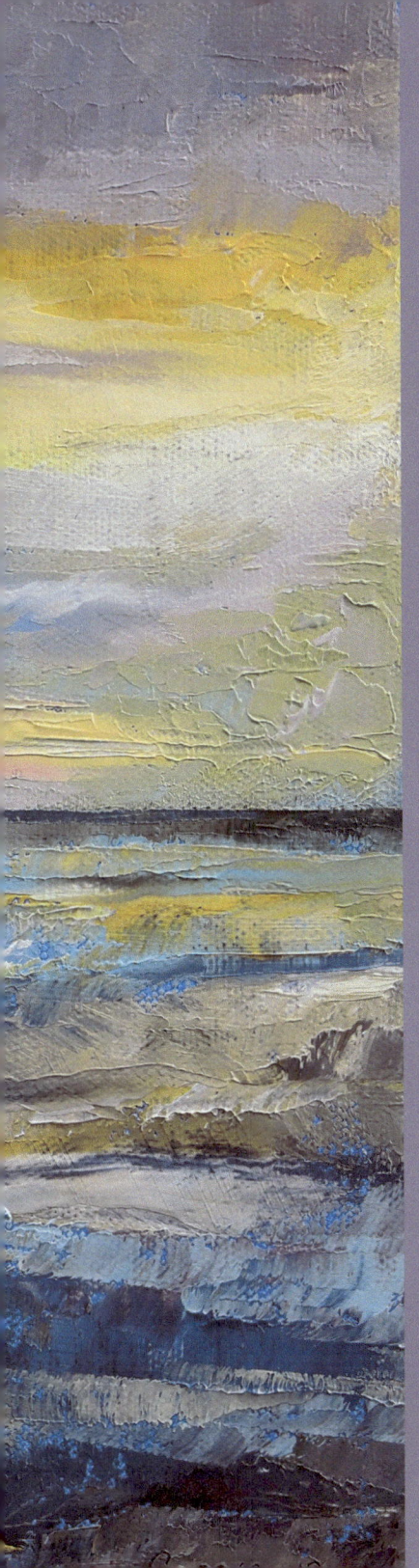

Damask patterns and lilac hues move out over the ocean, as graceful waves reflect a pastel sky over Bermuda.

A new beginning.

Part 3
Alluring

Tahitian sunsets never fail to amaze.

Not quite blue, and not quite green, perhaps somewhere in between? No Earthly color can match this shade.

One beautiful moment after another, day after day.

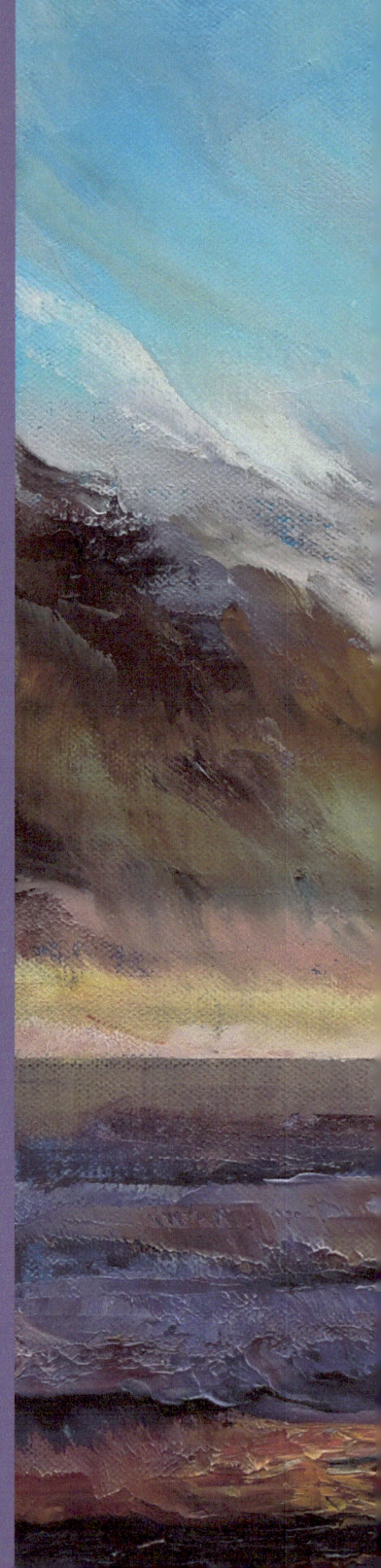

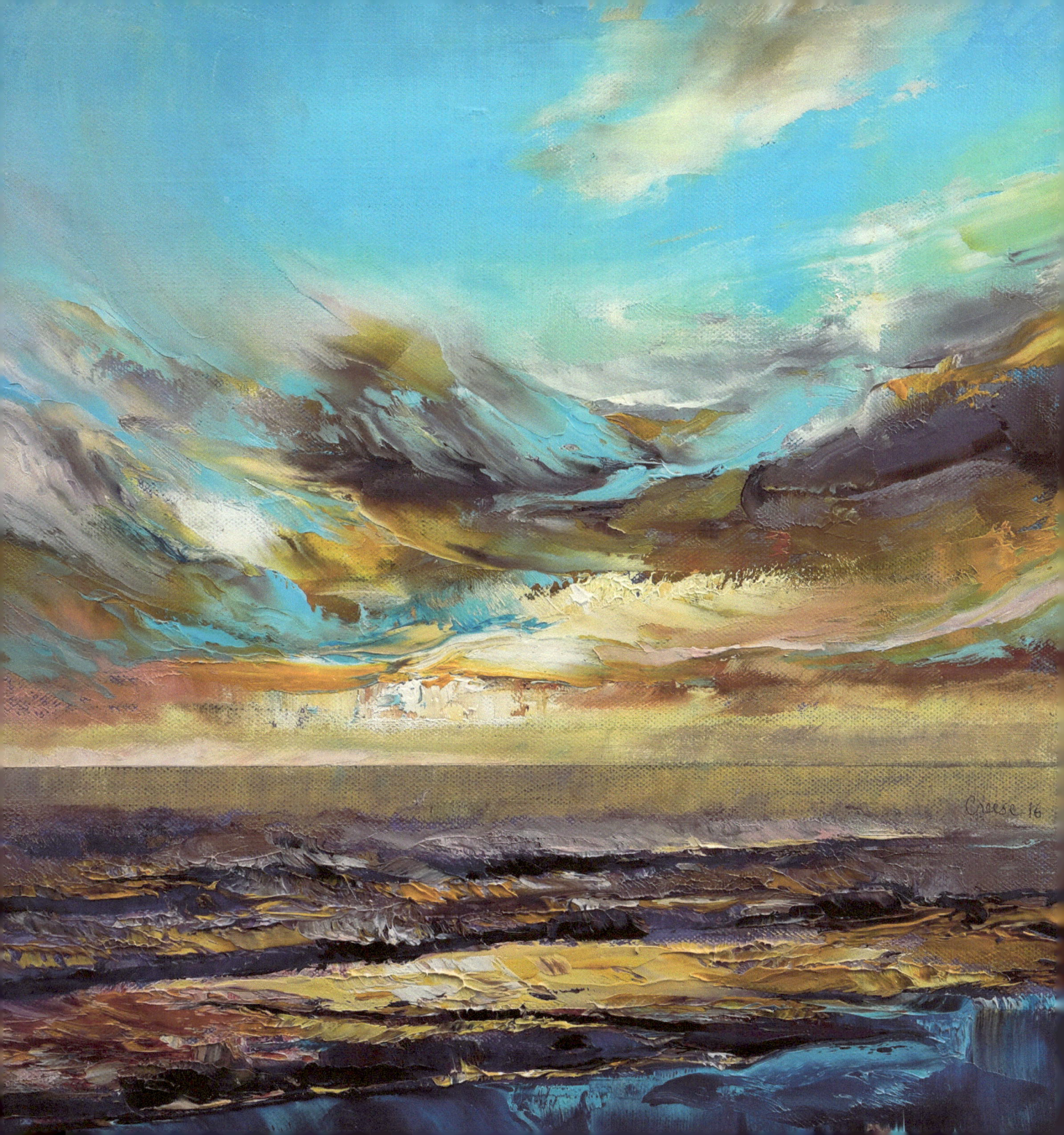

Malibu sunset with pale lavender clouds and infinite ocean waves.

The orange glow of the Sun is scalloped by sky blue and bright turquoise.

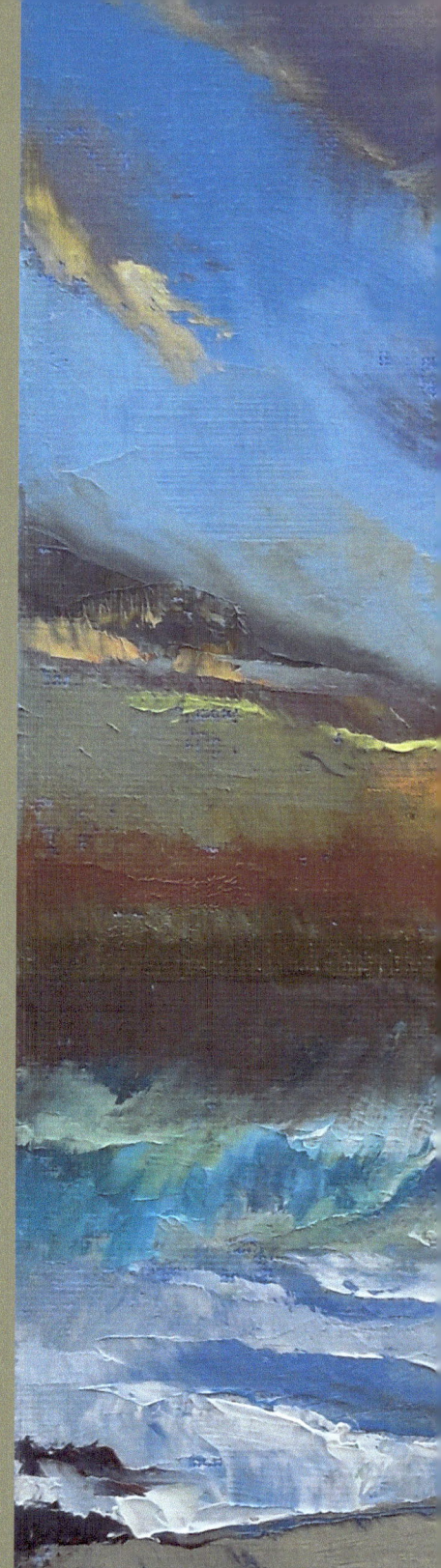

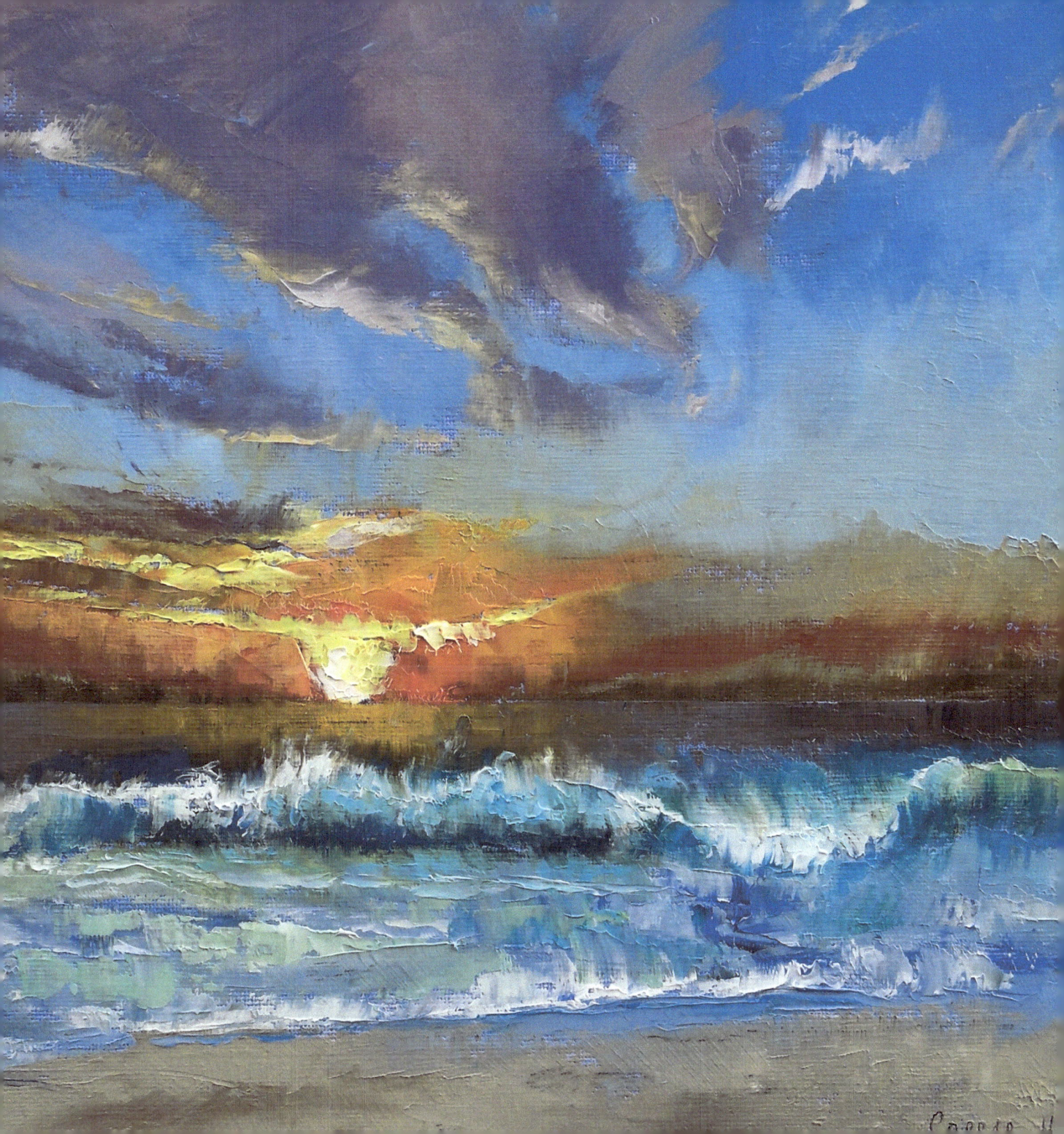

Islamorada sunset on a trip to the Florida Keys.

Only Nature can produce such beautiful sunsets.

A painter can try one's best to capture the beauty of this natural world, but it's never quite the same.

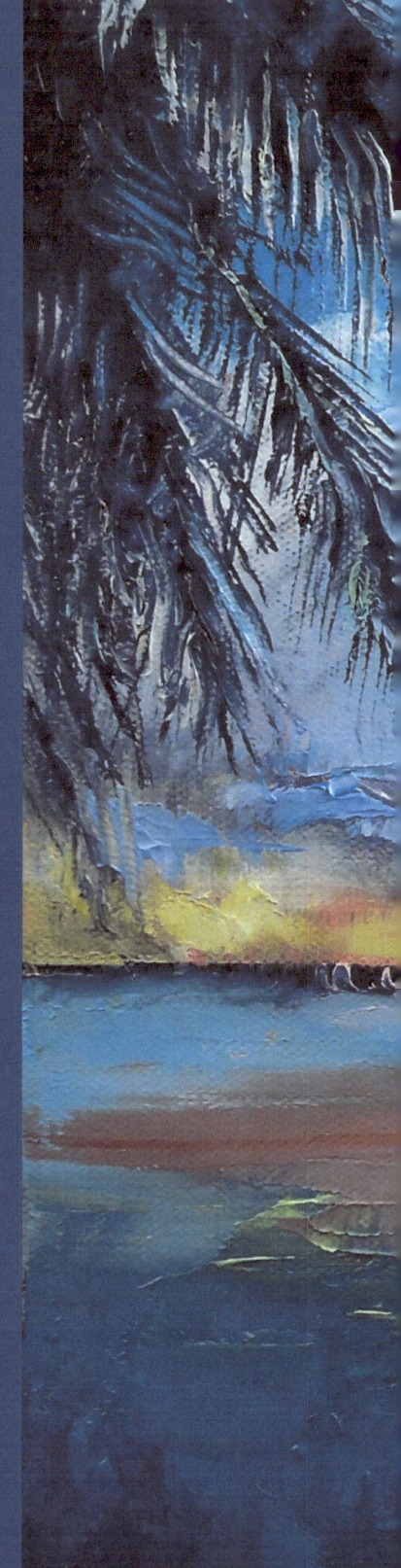

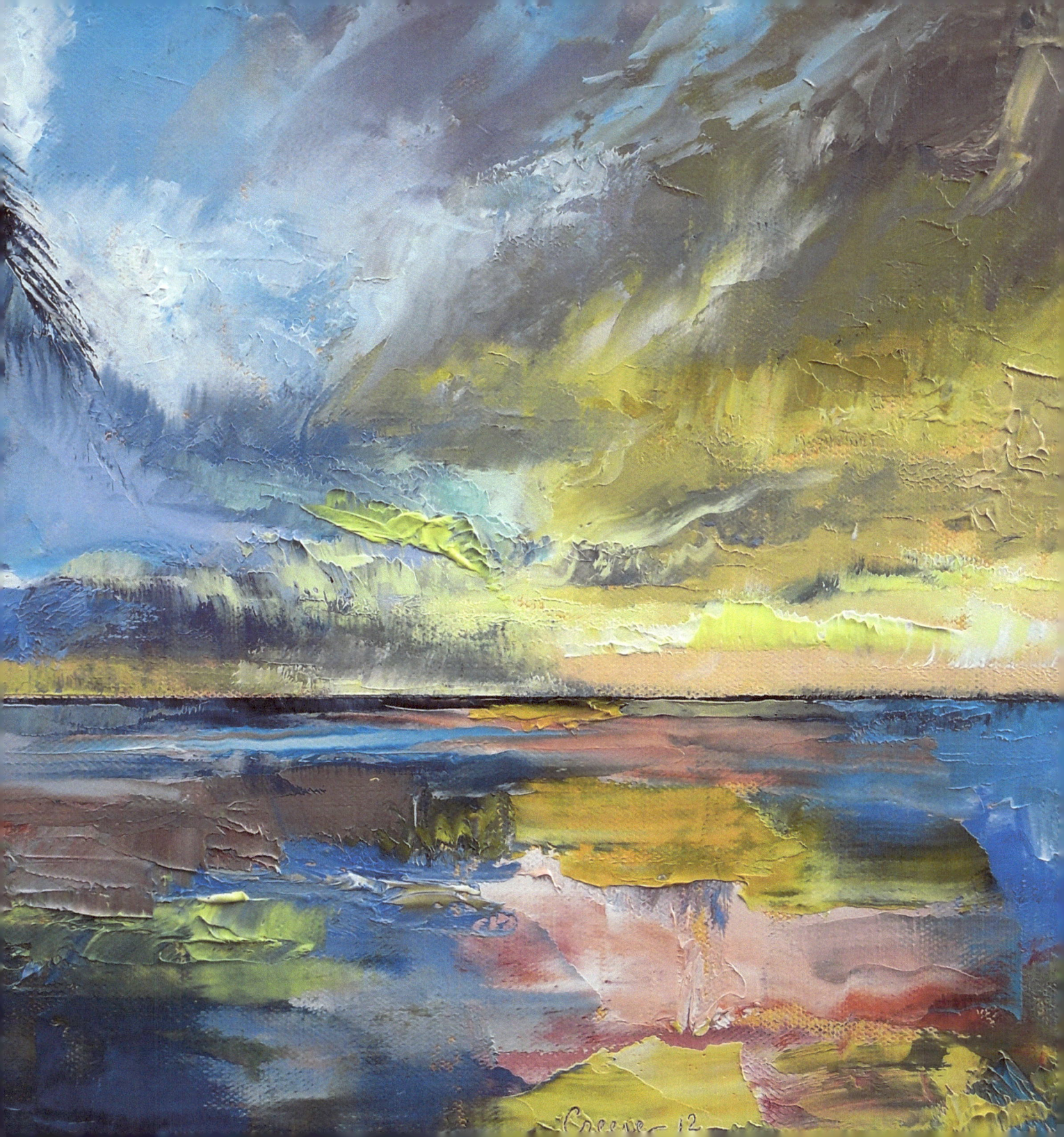

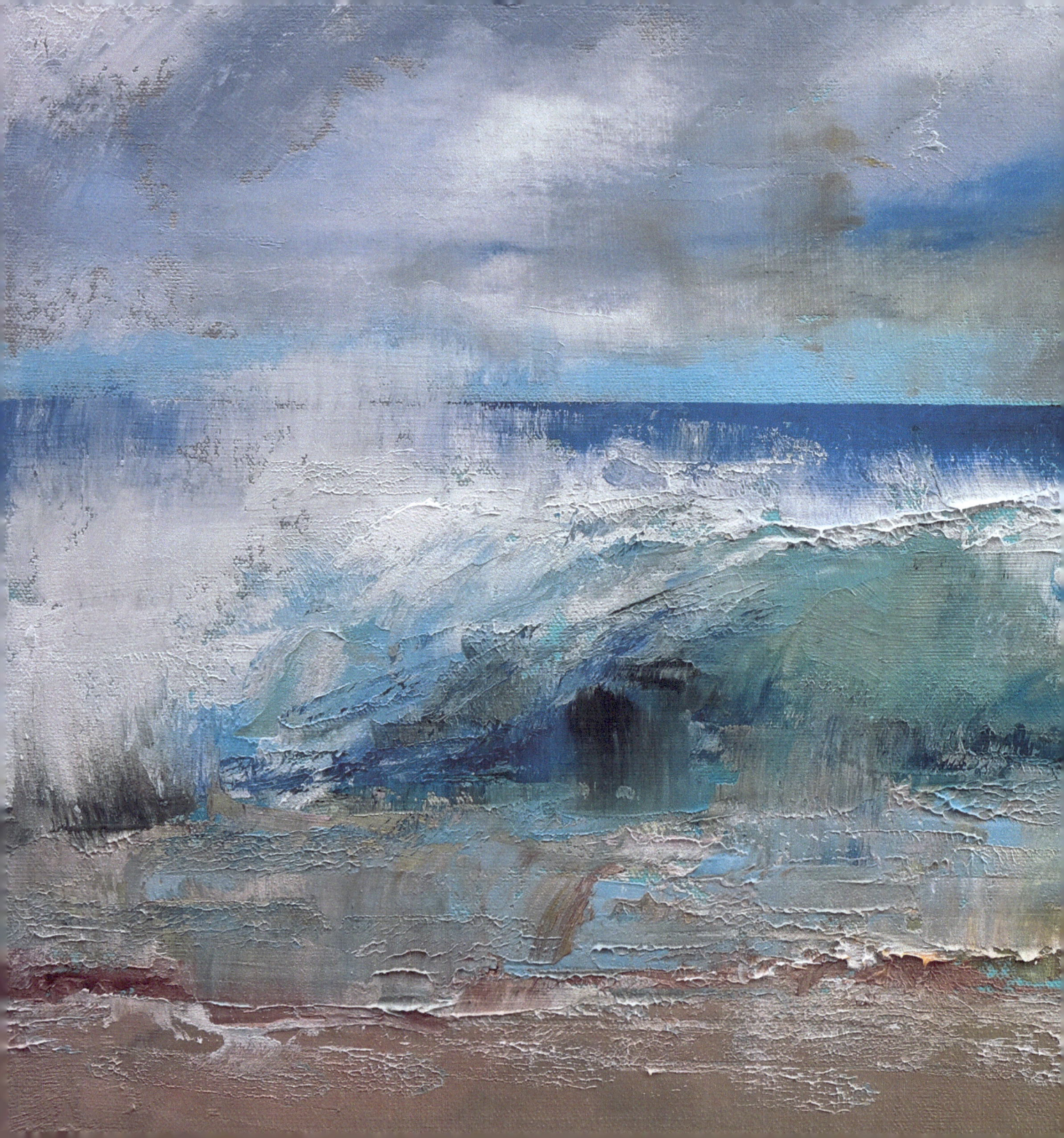

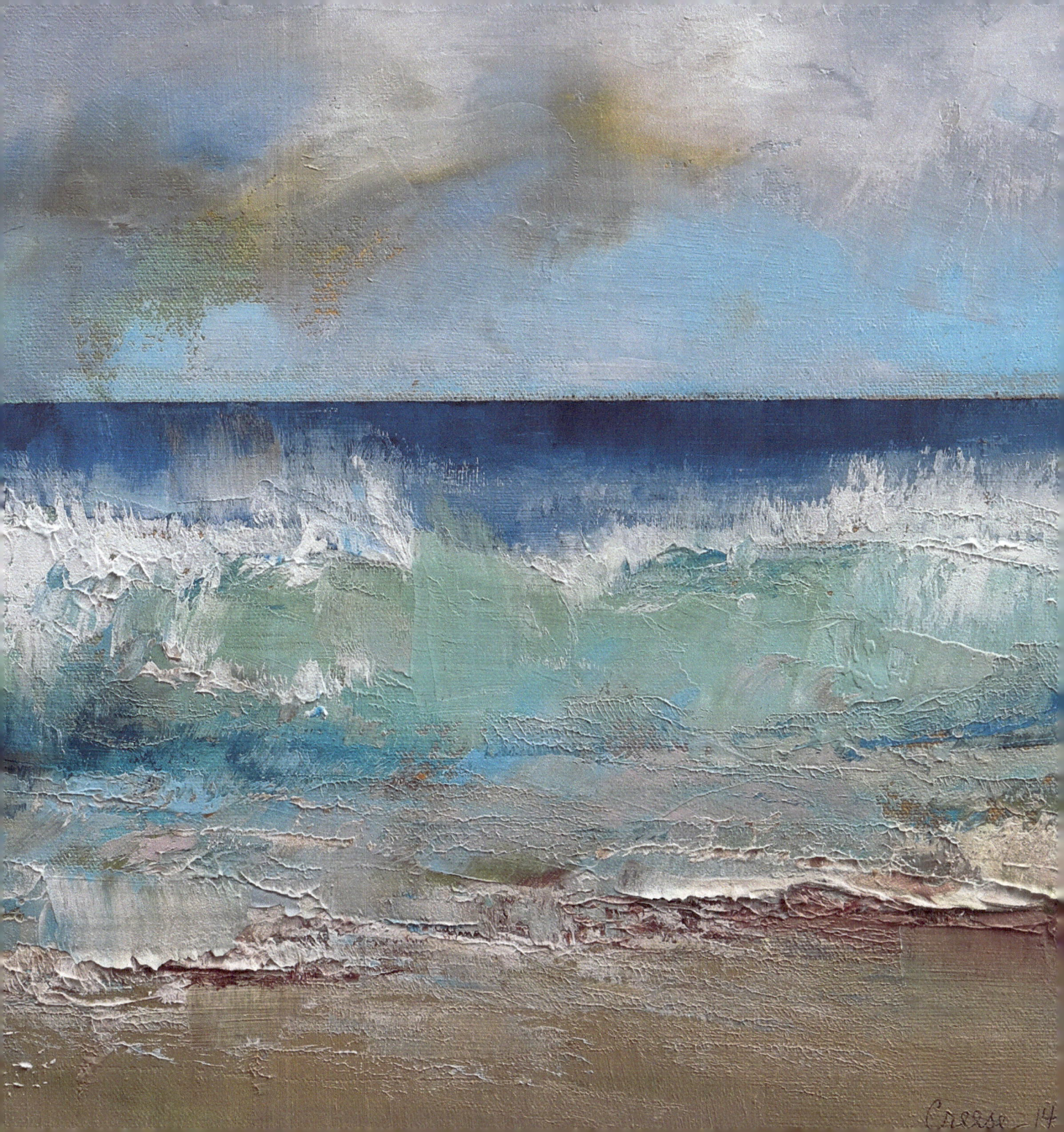

Storm clouds forming off the coast of the Galápagos Islands, create an immense stage.

A lone seagull, unfazed, follows a path through the gathering darkness.

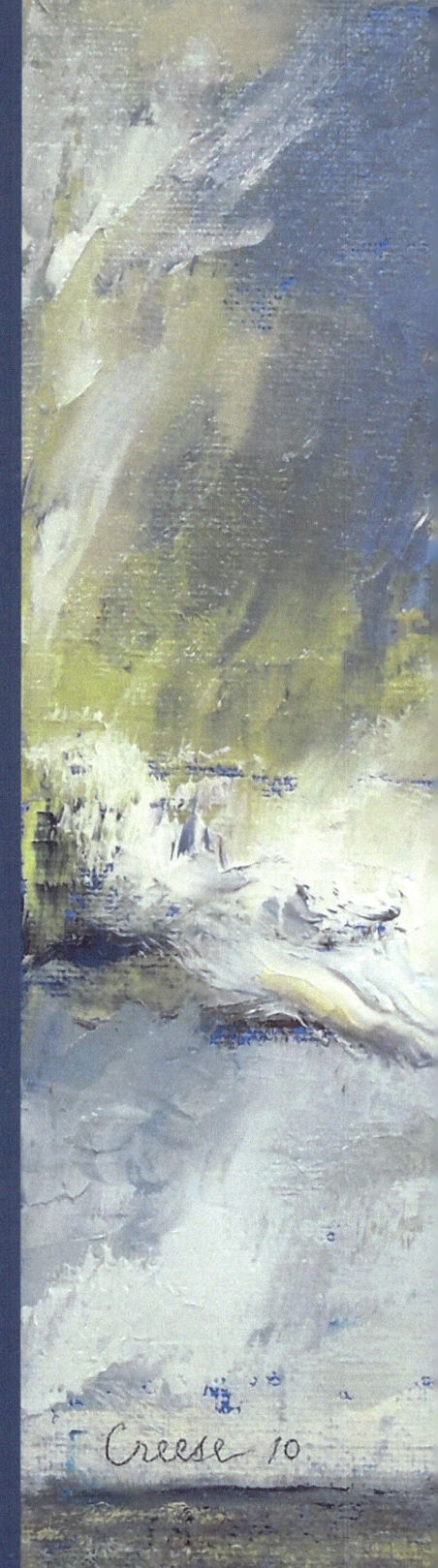

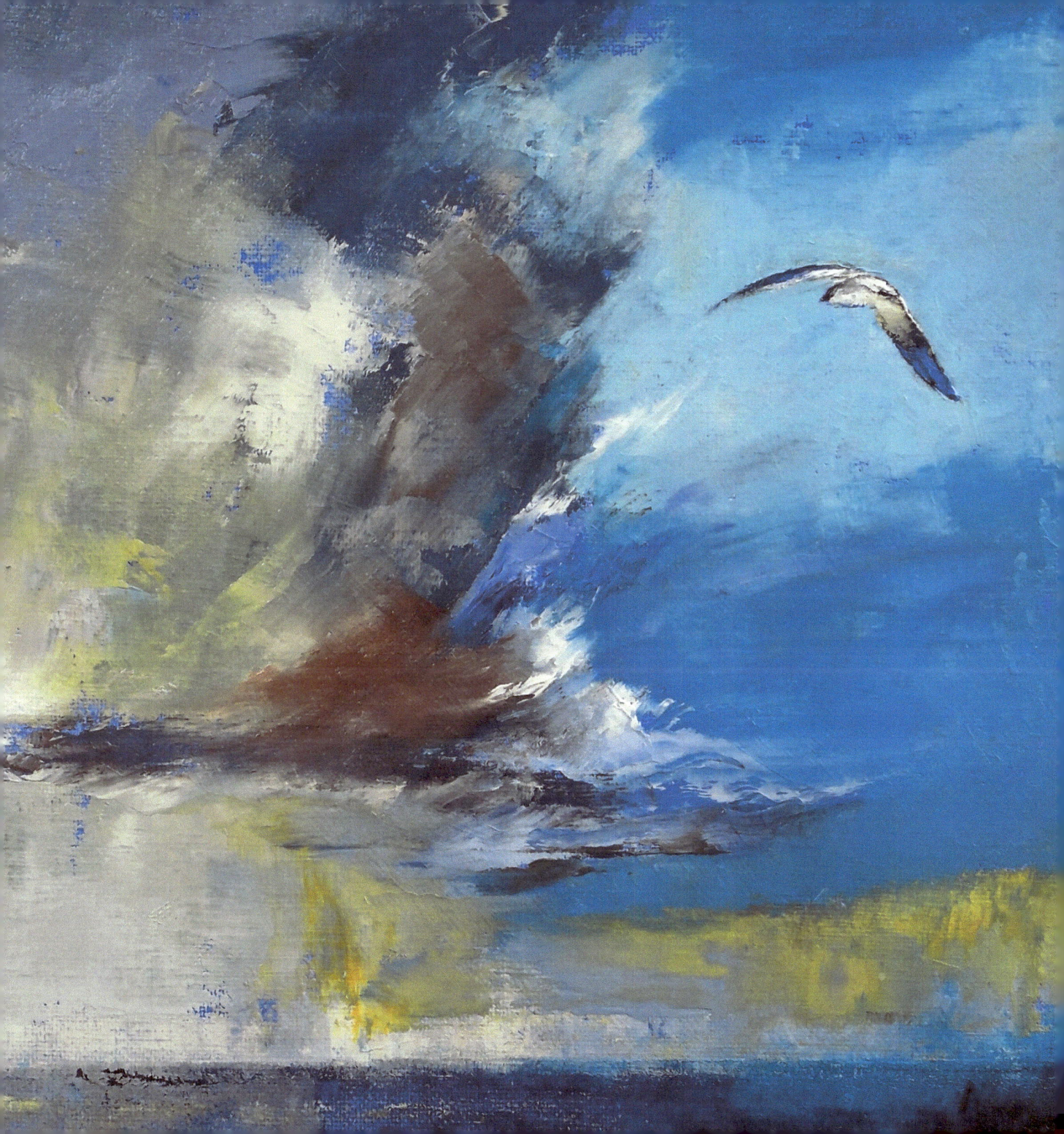

Emerald Isle, North Carolina sunset with waves inundating the shore, calling out like a rejected love.

The forms in the sky belie the expectations of the heart.

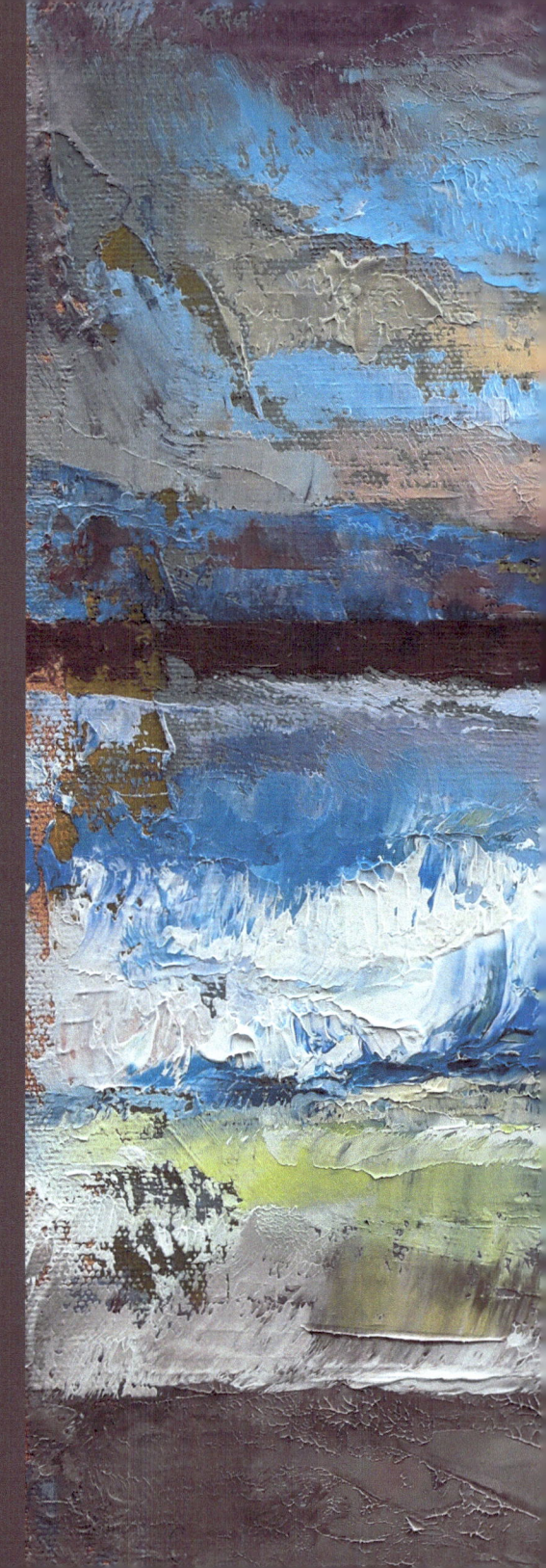

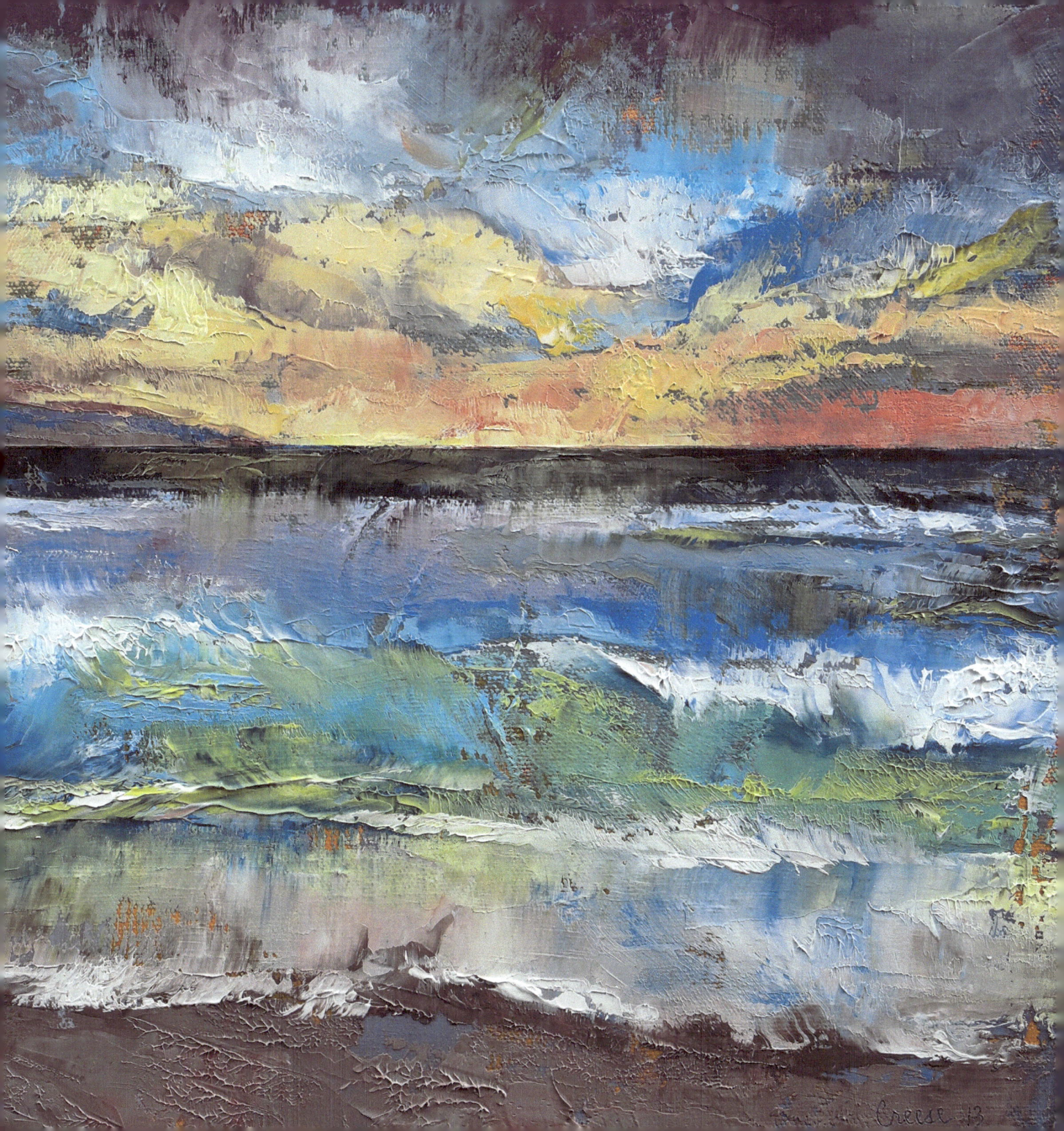

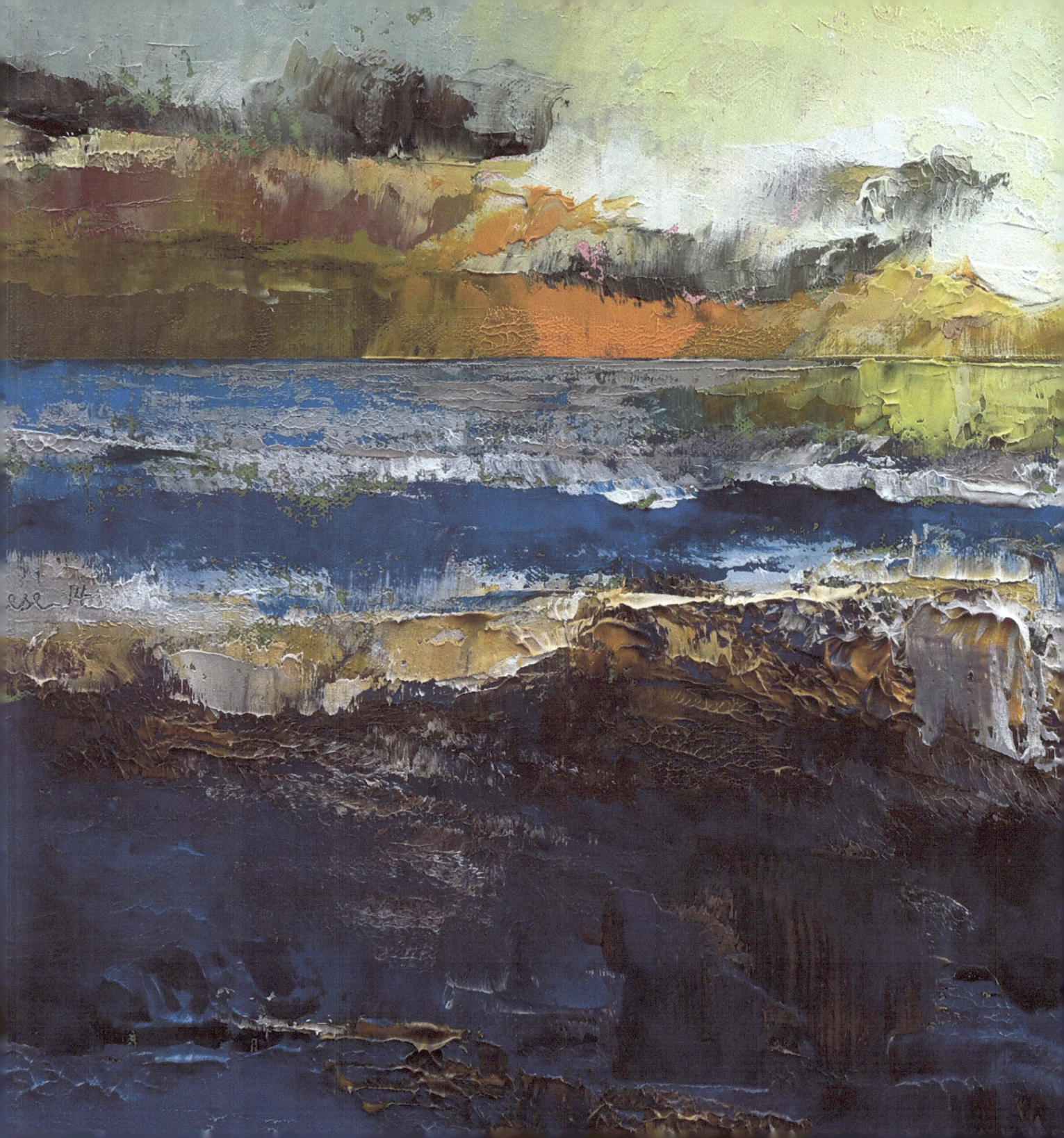

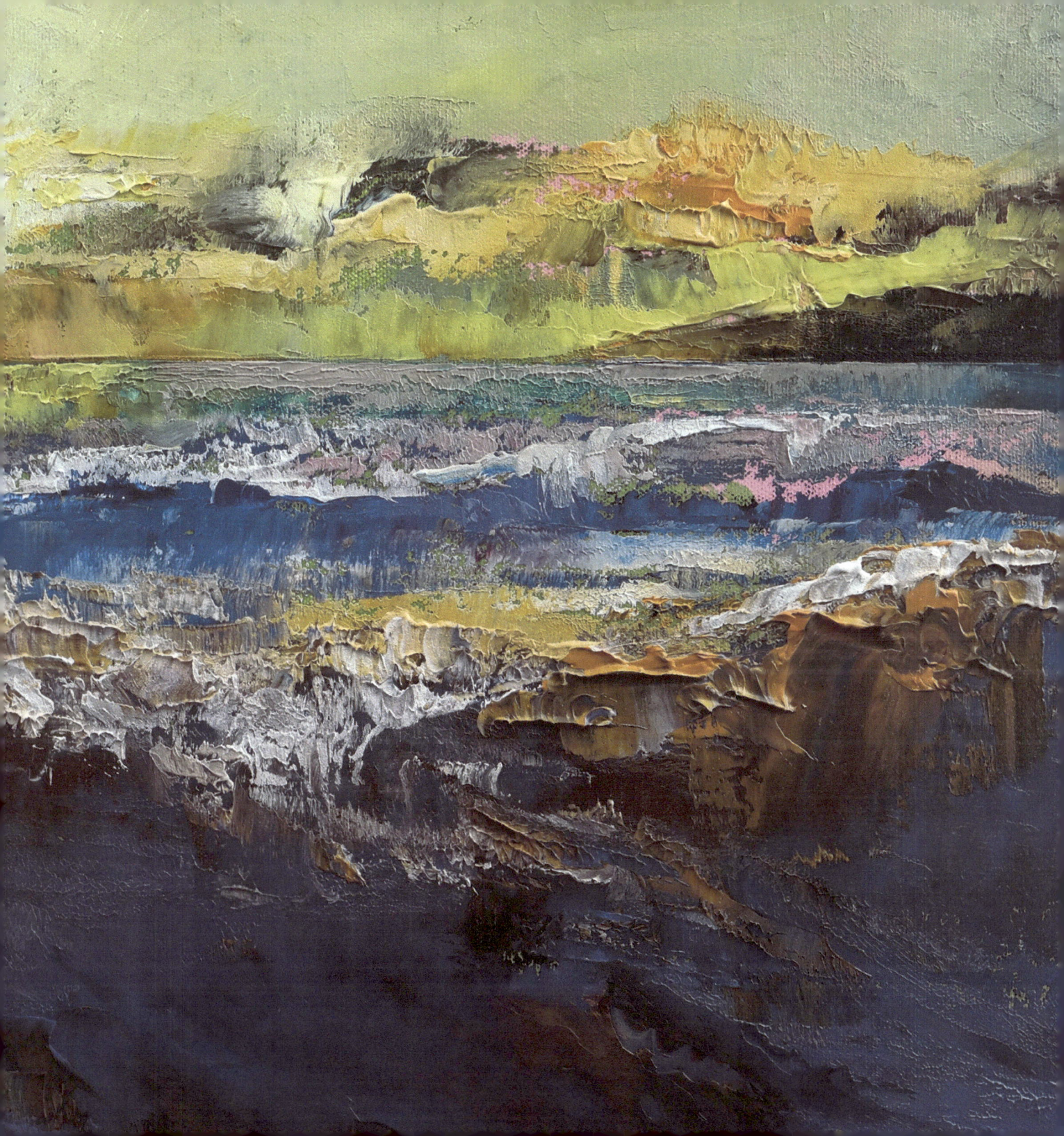

At last, the Moon rises silently over the ocean.

A refuge from the storm.

Lighting the ocean on the darkest nights.

This is home!

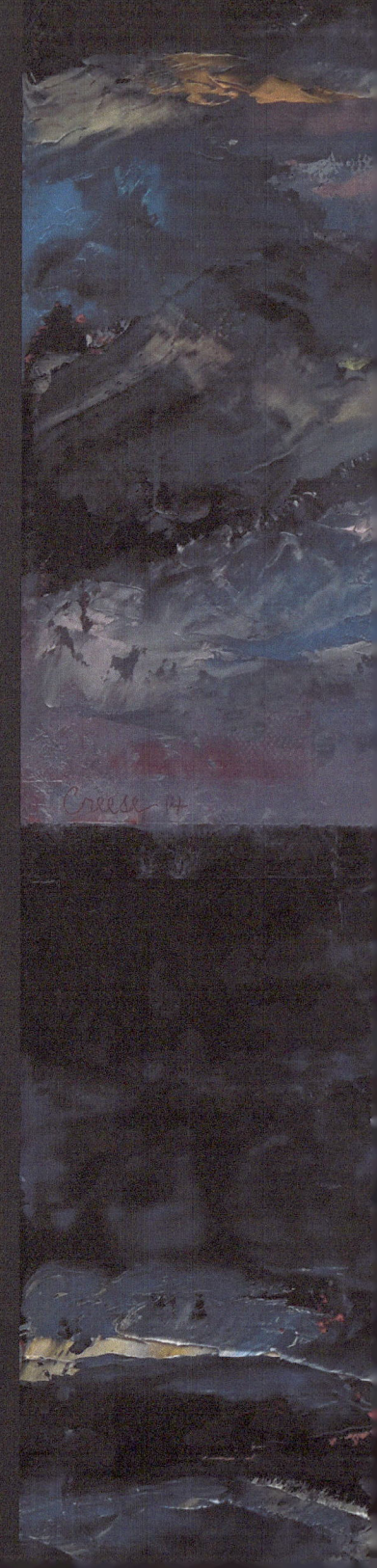

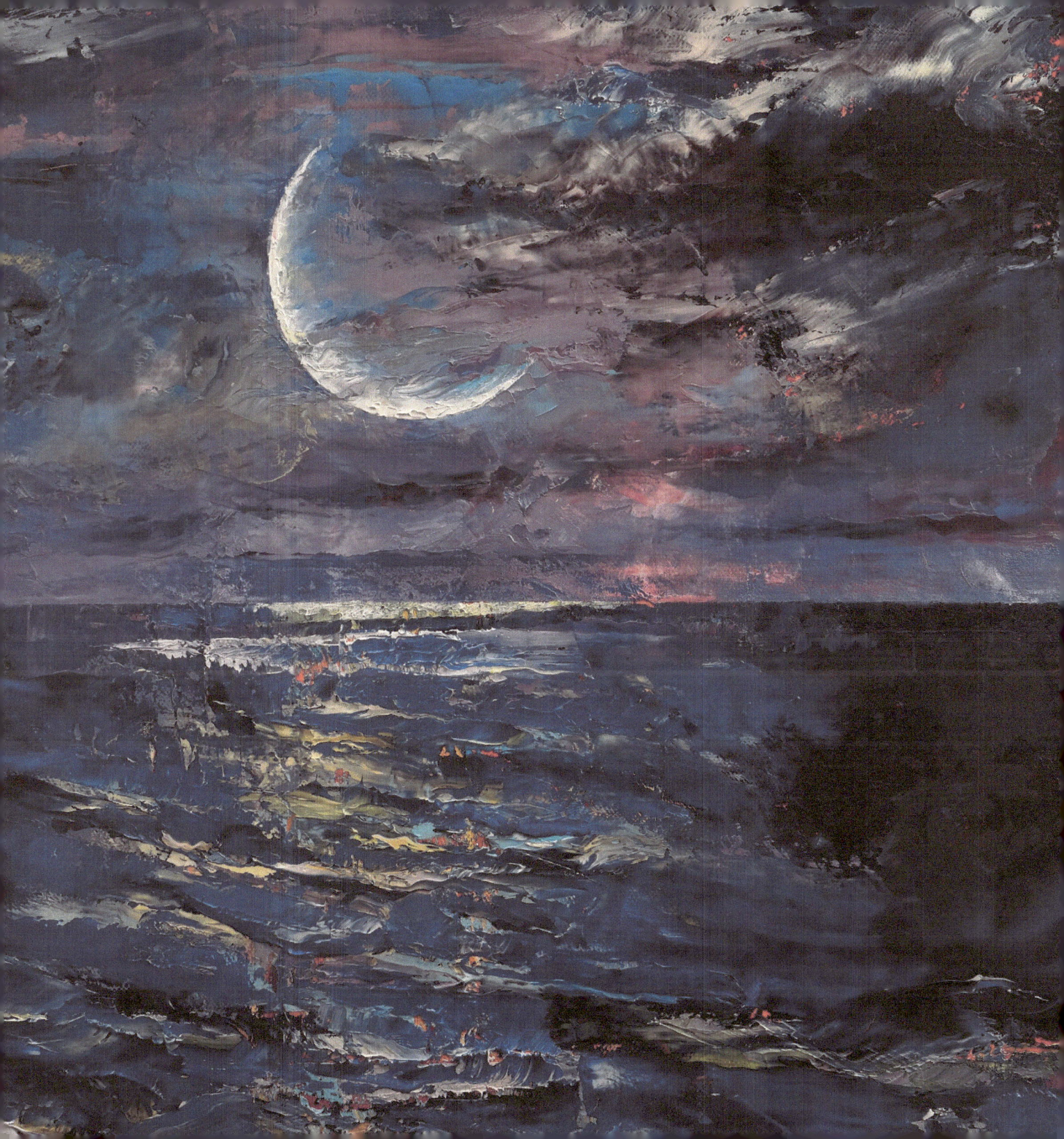

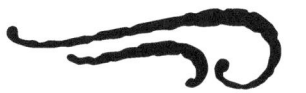

ABOUT THE AUTHOR

Michael Creese was born in Chicago, Illinois, and studied art at Carnegie Mellon University, where he received a Bachelor of Fine Arts degree.

He paints in the oil impasto style, a technique used in art where paint is laid thickly on canvas, leaving visible brush (or palette knife) strokes. When dry, impasto provides a great deal of texture to the finished painting. He also works with several other mediums in addition to oils.

You can find his art books and illustrations on Amazon.

www.michaelcreese.com

www.ingramcontent.com/pod-product-compliance
Lightning Source LLC
Chambersburg PA
CBHW051209220526
45473CB00003B/962